Early acclaim for
The Journey That Never Was

"Filled with Truth and inspiration throughout, this wonderful book brings insight and clarity to hearing God's Voice within you."

– James Twyman, author of *Emissary of Light*

"I highly recommend this powerful *Course in Miracles* related book to anyone and everyone who experiences difficulty in attempting to hear the Voice of God. I truly wish this book had been written when I first started the Course."

– Ron Rasmussen, Unity of Grand Rapids, MN

"I've shared with our church congregation that this is the best book I have read on HOW to be in communication with God. I couldn't put the book down because it was so easy to understand and such joyful reading. I liked the clarity in the explanations about God, the Holy Spirit, Jesus, God's Will, and Truth."

– Rev. Susan EngPoole, Unity of Louisville, KT

"DavidPaul and Candace Doyle have written the quintessential tool for reaching the Holy Spirit within each and every one of us. The format is delicious, with questions and answers from Holy Spirit and brief anecdotal references to their personal lives. I love it. It's like *A Course in Miracles for Dummies*!"

– Joy Poulter, Palm City, FL

"Having been an unrelenting student of *A Course In Miracles* for over twenty years, I have become quite confident in and comfortable with communicating with Spirit and hearing the Voice, but after reading this incredible book, my confidence grew exponentially and my comfort became reassurance."

– Rev. Tony Senf, Cleveland, OH

"For many of us, a direct communication from God through the Holy Spirit is improbable. We think too small of ourselves. We are fearful; or we are doubting, but needy. This book not only convinces us that it is possible, but that this communication is inevitable. If you are an occasional underliner of adages and pithy truths, get two pencils out because you will want to underline most of the book. It is that insightful and practical— truly transformative."

— John R. Fletcher, Bratenahl, OH

"DavidPaul and Candace Doyle offer a great gift ... proven methods to easily access and communicate with the ever present, loving, and wise Holy Spirit within you."

— Bob and Kathy Thompson, Portage, WI

"This book is a tremendously important spiritual work! It precipitated a long sought awakening for me."

— Rev. Jack Poole, Unity of Louisville, KT

"This is the first step-by-step practical guide that demystifies the communication process and makes hearing the Voice for God as natural and easy as talking on the phone."

— Karen Bentley, author of *The Book of Love*

"I wholeheartedly recommend this book to anyone seeking to access the Inner Voice of wisdom that we all share. Its guidance is offered through exercises, dialogue, and personal stories of the authors with warmth, humility, and clarity."

— Dennis Gaither, Mt. Vernon, WA

"There are a number of good *Course in Miracles* related books with much valuable information, but not all are easy to read. DavidPaul and Candace Doyle have done an excellent job of making this an interesting, even compelling read, as well as providing valuable tools for spiritual growth."

— Myron Jones, Lake Charles, LA

"This book is and will be very helpful to many people. I am so grateful that it has been published.... DavidPaul and Candace Doyle are mighty companions in the Plan, and their willingness to serve the Holy Spirit is graciously evident. May this book help many to open to the Voice for God within and thus fulfill their role in the Great Awakening."
                                        – David Hoffmeister, Cincinnati, OH

"Some of the concepts tackled so brilliantly in this book can be made to seem very complicated to us. Our egos assure us that to 'get it' will be a long and arduous task. *The Journey That Never Was*, in straight forward language, spells out a gentle path to helping us realize who we really are. The highlights brought out at the end of each chapter drive home the important message this book delivers."
                                        – Jack Barney, Eugene, OR

"This book empowers each of us to receive the gift of the Voice for God in our own way. It's an easy, delightful, and truly inspiring read. I recommend it highly!"
                                        – Rev. Jill Sabin Carel, *Agape Interfaith Ministries*

"DavidPaul and Candace Doyle are brilliant in their methods and practices regarding spirituality. I regard this book as a must read and a wonderful guide to living in Truth. What a gift!"
                                        – Rev. Lee Poepping, Santa Clarita Unity Church

"An inspiring look into the many ways of opening to the Inner Voice of the Holy Spirit that is within all of us. I have recommended this book to all of my *A Course in Miracles* students."
                                        – Rev. Dr. Diane Michele, Warren, MI

"I have been a student of *A Course in Miracles* for 16 years. *The Journey That Never Was* lent a clarity that had been missing up until now. It is an easy read and contains well-written directions for accessing your inner connection. It really should be required reading."
                                        – Vivian Miller, Garfield, OH

The Journey
That Never Was

The Journey
That Never Was

✦

A guide to hearing God's Voice regardless
of one's faith, religion, or personal beliefs

DavidPaul and Candace Doyle

Foundation for Right-Mindedness
New York Ashland Shanghai

The Journey That Never Was
A guide to hearing God's Voice regardless of one's faith, religion, or personal beliefs

Publisher's Cataloging-in-Publication
(Provided by Quality Books, Inc.)

Doyle, DavidPaul.
  The journey that never was : a guide to hearing God's voice regardless of one's faith, religion, or personal beliefs / DavidPaul and Candace Doyle.
  p. cm.
  LCCN 2005925024
  ISBN 0-9766613-0-6
  ISBN 0-9766613-1-4

  1. Spiritual life. 2. Holy Spirit.   I. Doyle, Candace. II. Title.

BL624.D695 2005   204
                    QBI05-600005

Foundation books may be ordered through wholesalers, retailers, and by contacting:

Foundation for Right-Mindedness
PO Box 3125
Ashland, OR 97520
www.rightmindedness.com
(541) 488-0426

ISBN: 0-9766613-0-6
Printed in the United States of America

For You, God's One and only beloved Child

"The holy meeting place of the
unseparated Father and His Son
lies in the Holy Spirit and in You."

A Course in Miracles

Contents

Part II   Hearing God's Voice

Part III   Living With God's Voice

Acknowledgements

Writing this book is the fulfillment of one dream and the beginning of a new one. We would first like to thank the Holy Spirit for being God's Voice in the world and for all of the support, guidance, and inspiration we received in writing this book.

We would also like to thank our parents, Kit and Karl Schneider, Mike and Pauline Doyle, and Steve Kane, for the love and support they have given us while we've been walking a path they haven't always understood.

DavidPaul would especially like to thank his mother, DeeDee Davidson, for her courage and passion for Truth, which has been a source of inspiration to him this lifetime.

In addition, we would like to thank Anita Grimm, Sharon Williams, and Mark Scarpaci for their invaluable editorial feedback and Diane Youngs, Matty Z, and Wendy Moore for their loving support and encouragement.

Finally, we are very grateful to our family and friends who have loved and supported us on this journey, especially our daughter, Hannah, who continues to inspire us to be our best and who is an incredible reflection of the Truth of who we are.

About This Book

Hearing God's Voice is not a gift given to a rare few. We each have this Voice within us. Learning to hear It is not only teachable, but inevitable. *The Journey That Never Was* is a guide to hearing God's Voice within you, not in some esoteric or mystical way, but in a way that is just as real as picking up the phone and actually hearing God's Voice on the other end.

In 1994, while reading *A Course in Miracles*, Candace spontaneously started hearing the Voice of the Holy Spirit within her as a discernible, audible, conversational Voice. Her husband, DavidPaul, began hearing this Voice several years later after following exercises he was given by the Holy Spirit to help him hear this Voice for himself. Individually and as a married couple, we have sought guidance and support from this Voice for the past 10 years.

The goal of this book is to help *you* hear God's Voice within you. It is not intended to be an all encompassing resource for Truth or answer all of your questions. It is designed to give you the understanding and know-how to hear this Voice for yourself so that *you* can access all Truths within you and discover your own path for living in the world.

Throughout the book, we pose questions to the Holy Spirit to help build a framework for you to hear this Voice. We interweave exercises to deepen these concepts and ignite this Voice within you, and we also include our personal experiences of hearing and using this Voice over the years.

There are as many beliefs about God as there are people in the world, and even within one person, these beliefs can change depending on the day or what's going on in their life. *Part One* is designed to give you a framework for believing you are capable of hearing this Voice. *Part Two* discusses the barriers to hearing God's Voice and provides a number of methods for overcoming these barriers. It also includes chapters on meditation and prayer and culminates with a variety of exercises for hearing God's Voice within you. *Part Three* concludes the book with guidance about living with God's Voice in the world.

In this book, all communications from the Holy Spirit are identified by using quotations. In addition, *for the sake of simplification*, the word "He" is used in reference to God, rather than She, He/She, It, and so on, with the belief that God is neither male nor female. In all cases, the communications from the Holy Spirit were originally spoken, recorded, and then transcribed. While some messages have been slightly altered to make the conversational nature of the communication more readable, every attempt was made to leave the communications unaltered from their original delivery.

While it is our intention that this book will help you have everything you need to clearly hear this Voice within you, it is not necessary to agree with or believe the words in this book to more fully bring this Voice into your life. Take from these words what you will...what speaks to you in your heart...and know that God's Voice is with you every step of the way.

How This Book Came to Be

Candace: Like so many others, I have spent this lifetime searching. The most consistent thing my family has said about me over the years is "there she goes again," which meant I was beginning another adventure in search of the Truth. Along the way, I discovered many helpful practices and concepts, but none of them fulfilled my need for Truth over the long run.

Then one morning, while doing a lesson from *A Course in Miracles* (ACIM) and meditating for a long time afterward, I heard a Voice in my head tell me to surrender. I wasn't the type to surrender, and not to a voice in my head, so I said no. Again this Voice asked me to surrender and again I said no. This went on for a while until finally, and I don't know why, I surrendered. In that instant a loving and knowing Voice flowed into me and filled me with the most beautiful message about myself that I had ever heard. I asked this Voice who It was, and It told me that It was the Holy Spirit, which was the Voice for God, God's Translator and Comforter in the world.

The Lesson I was doing that day in ACIM was "In quiet I receive God's Word today." This lesson was about hearing God's Voice within. It said, ".... He speaks from nearer than your heart to you. His Voice is closer than your hand. His Love is everything you are and that He is; the same as you, and you the same as He. It is your voice to which you listen as He speaks to you. It is your Word He speaks. It is the Word of freedom and of peace, of unity of will and purpose, with no separation nor division in the single Mind of Father and of Son. In quiet listen to your Self today, and let Him tell you God has never left His Son, and you have never left your Self...."

Discovering God's Voice that day ended my search for Truth. I found the Truth within me, where It had been all along. I have since spent the last ten years learning Who the Holy Spirit is and coming to understand that we each have this Voice within us, that It is part of us and cannot be separate from us no matter what we might think or say or do. No one is more worthy than another of hearing God's Voice, nor is it a special gift given to a rare few.

The Holy Spirit has told me that my function is to teach others how to hear this Voice for themselves. As such, I am like a public relations person for the Holy Spirit, Who was created by God as the answer to our misperceptions, as the wake-up call to our long sleep, as the Guide on our journey that never was. The Holy Spirit knows that the journey never was, but until we realize this completely for ourselves, He will join us where we are and guide us in whatever ways we need to find our way Home. And even this will be done only at our request, when we are ready.

DavidPaul: I had a wonderful childhood. I feel fortunate that my early memories are only of playing and having fun. Though I was baptized Catholic as a young boy and attended Sunday school, Catholicism wasn't a central theme in my family. Going to church was just something we did on holidays and special occasions. We were a typical middle-class family, doing what everyone else did, trying to move ahead in the world and enjoy our lives as best we could. This all changed the day my mother met a woman who channeled an energy known as Demetrius from the Great White Brotherhood. I was eight years old at the time.

My mother was instantly attracted to the messages she heard from the Brotherhood about reincarnation and being a spirit. I too was drawn to what they were saying and listened to their sessions with fascination whenever I could. The words that I heard felt true, inspiring, and very reassuring, and from that point on, I held a deep sense within me that I was more than my body.

As I entered the ninth grade, my carefree life came to a screeching halt. My parents divorced, and when they did, a fire was ignited within me for the first time in my life to become something more than I was. At 15 years old, the highest attainment I could envision for myself was John Glenn, a celebrated astronaut and United States Senator....It was here that my journey began.

I wrote the Senator a letter asking how I could follow in his footsteps. With his suggestion that I attend the U.S. Air Force Academy, I went to the library, checked out the Academy's submission guidelines, and then charted every class, extracurricular activity, and step I would need to take to get accepted. Filled with passion and determination to accomplish this goal, I worked very hard for the next three years. I was eventually accepted into the Academy, and in the summer of 1987, ready and raring to go, I flew to Colorado Springs, CO to become a cadet.

I loved being at the Academy. I enjoyed the games, the challenges, the camaraderie, the sense of purpose, and as I did in high school, I planned out every move I needed to make to become who I wanted to be. Toward the end of my sophomore year, everything was going as planned, until an unexpected event happened in my life.

It was a month before the first day of my junior year, which was the day all cadets must sign their military commitment. I was listening to Kenny G. on the radio, and about half way through the song, an explosion erupted within me. My heart opened and a wave of love came over me. It felt as if the love had come from Kenny G. himself—that somehow he had packaged up the love within himself and placed it into his music for all to receive. It was the most powerful experience of love I had ever felt.

Filled with joy and wonder, a life-changing question came to mind: "If I was an old man on my deathbed, how would I have lived my life to have had absolutely no regrets?"

I contemplated this question and came to the realization that what I wanted more than anything else in the world was to share the gift of love that I had just received.

I then thought, "How on earth would I do that?"

Searching for an answer within me, I saw a vision in my mind of a book that impacted people's lives in a profound way, all over the world. I had no idea what the book would say or how I would write it, but I knew in that moment that staying in the military was not going to take me there.

When the semester ended, I sped away on a motorcycle and never returned. Since then, my life has taken many unexpected twists and turns, and what started out as a quest to become more than I was has now transformed into a passion for being who I already am.

May you receive the love that we have packaged up within these pages, and may this love inspire you to live the Truth of who you are in the world.

DavidPaul and Candace Doyle
Ashland, OR
October, 2004

PART I

Remembering God's Voice

"The Truth is within each of God's children.
It is a journey, rather than a destination,
that begins with a thought rather than a step."

1

The Holy Spirit

"The Holy Spirit offers that which you truly seek,
contentedness, peace, love,
and the constant reminder of who you really are."

Holy Spirit: "God loves His Child so much that He wanted His Child to always know that It is safe, It is loved, and It is whole. God created the Holy Spirit as a way to ensure that God's Child would always know these things. God gave the Holy Spirit to His Child, and the Holy Spirit is now a part of that Child. It is the eternal perspective of Truth, Love, and Reality that cannot be taken from that Child. It is the Voice of God instilled within and the ever-present reminder to that Child of the Truth of Who and What It is and the love Its Father has for It."

Who is the Holy Spirit?

Candace: Who is the Holy Spirit and what is the Holy Spirit's relationship to the ego?

Holy Spirit: "Once upon a non-time, there was God. Then God's Child, an aspect of God, a part of the whole, had the thought that it could do something on its own, that somehow it could be separate from the whole. In that instant the ego was made, which is ultimately just a way of thinking that supports that part of God in believing that it is separate from the whole. That is all the ego is, and the only purpose it fulfills is the constant reminder of the illusion that that piece of God is separate from its Oneness, that there is no Oneness, and that it is on its own.

"As God noticed this aspect of Itself holding this thought and saw the ego coming alive to reinforce that thought, God simultaneously created the Holy Spirit, not as a counter to the ego, but as a cure—to hold Truth within the mind as well, so that either would be available at any given time. There cannot be an opposite to what does not exist, but there can be a Truth to prove the inexistence of what is not, and that is the relationship of the Holy Spirit to the ego.

"God, in His Perfection, is not capable of recognizing the ego and the errors in thinking that go with the ego, yet God can be aware of a need in His Child. God had the understanding that at some point that aspect of Itself would tire of the thought that It is separate from the whole, and when It did, when It became so tired from that thought, It would have the Holy Spirit to gently guide it back to the Truth of its Oneness.

"The ego has a full-time job holding the perspective that one can be separate from its Creator. The ego's full-time job is to convince you that you are on your own, alone, roaming the world, and that you are never truly connected, united, or one with anything. You may be born into a family, and yet that family will come and go. You may form a marriage, and that marriage will come and go. You may have children, and they will come and go. You are never ultimately at one with anything, no matter what you do to try to attain that. That is the ego's number one job. The ego might even discourage you from having unity with your family, a true sense of union in your marriage, and a deep connection with your children to reaffirm your aloneness and your separation. The ego is diligent, hardworking, and loyal to its purpose. It will fight to the end to do its job to convince you that you are separate.

"The Holy Spirit is ever patient and vigilant in its belief about your Oneness. The Holy Spirit cannot intrude upon your dream and attempt to wake you up before your sleep is done, but the Holy Spirit never leaves your side, watching over you, loving you, and reassuring you that ultimately there will be a happy ending.

"By creating the Holy Spirit, God created a way to bring His Voice into each of His children as they go out into the world so that they could always remember the Truth of who and what they are. The Holy Spirit's function and purpose is to bring God's Voice to each of God's children, guiding them, directing them, loving them, and restoring their thinking to Right-Mindedness and Truth. Truth is the bridge to God.

"Little by little, as you hear, recognize, understand, and become aware of the Holy Spirit in different ways—through your thinking, through correcting a thought with the Holy Spirit, through recognizing the Holy Spirit in another, through sharing the Words of the Holy Spirit with someone, through hearing the Holy Spirit in another when they speak, and so on—the Holy Spirit is brought into the world and given to each of God's children, recognized in each of God's children, and used as a reminder for God's children of the Truth so that they can overcome the world.

"The Holy Spirit was given to each of God's children by God, put within each one, and is now a part of them. It is not to think that the Holy Spirit is separate from you, is really only a part of God, or will one day be separate because, in Truth, the Holy Spirit is now part of you. It has now been blended and melted into you. That is why it is important to recognize the Holy Spirit in everyone you meet because the Holy Spirit is a part of them, and in the world the Holy Spirit represents your connectedness, your family ties to God.

"The Holy Spirit is within each of God's children and cannot be extracted. It is there as a constant resource, companion, and speaker of Truth no matter what you think you have done, what you think you are doing, and what you think you might do. The Holy Spirit holds no judgments, never condemns, and only remembers your true Perfection. In that is the impossibility of sin or anything related to it.

"It is not possible for the Holy Spirit to judge you in any way because the Holy Spirit can only see the Truth of who you are and not who you think you are. The Holy Spirit can also see who you think you are and not believe it. The Holy Spirit can see what you think and does not join you on that sinking ship. The Holy Spirit only knows one Truth and that is your Perfection, regardless of your insistence to prove otherwise. The Holy Spirit cannot join you in any thinking about yourself other than your Perfection, though the Holy Spirit can love you while you think insane thoughts.

"When you are suffering, it is because of the belief in separation while simultaneously having the hope of Oneness. There is the hope but not the proof, and then there is fear and suffering. The Holy Spirit is within your mind and is ever available to you to restore your thinking to Truth. In any moment that you decide that you do not want to participate in the belief of separation—if you decide you want peace, if you decide you want to remember who you are and what you are—the Holy Spirit is there waiting to join with you in Truth. The Holy Spirit has been within you since your first step into the world and offers you an alternative to pain and suffering, to fear and loathing, to vengeance and death. The Holy Spirit offers Peace, Oneness, Truth and everlasting Life.

"The ego, on the other hand, has invented all of the thinking that would have you believe in the body. There is the idea that the body is the temple of the Holy Spirit—that alone may be one of the bigger misconceptions going. The body is the temple of the ego in the sense that everything that is temporary is made by the ego. Everything that is eternal is created by God. The ego is temporary. The body is temporary.

"If you see another person in the world and think anything of them other than that they are a beloved and whole Child of God, then that is the ego feeding you that thought. The only Truth about the one in front of you is, 'There is God's beloved and holy Child.'

"As you come across the people in the world, the ego would convince you that this one is this and this one is that and that one is this and the judgments go on and on and on, and none of that is True. The world is made out of the thoughts of the ego. God did not make the world. The thoughts of the ego made the world. You may look upon the world and think it is a beautiful place, certain areas are beautiful, certain things are beautiful, certain people are beautiful, but if you cannot look upon the world and see that all of it is beautiful, then you are looking through the eyes of the ego.

"If you look upon the world and see fear, loathing, hatred, separation, death, or destruction, these are what the ego would convince you are happening in the world to keep you in fear and to keep you distracted from God. If you were to overcome the beliefs that you have about the body, that alone would change everything. As long as you believe that you *are* the body—you need the body, you are dependent upon it, you need its health, you need its well being, you need its limbs, you need its mental faculties, and so on—you are in quicksand. God's Hand is stretched out to you, but the more you struggle in your beliefs of what you have been told about the body, the deeper you sink. And God's Hand is waiting to pull you out at all times.

"The ego would have you believe that there are special relationships, such as families, lovers, children, friends, and other special people in your life. Though if you do not see all people as equal, then you are being deceived from seeing the Truth that everyone upon the earth is a Child of God and that you do not have a special relationship with any of them but in fact have a Union with all of them because each one of God's Children is part of your Oneness.

"When each one is not received in that way, then you deny yourself Oneness. Anytime you act in a way that you do not like, that you do not feel is loving or kind, anytime you act in a way that is as a result of fear or control, anything that is other than understanding and accepting, it is of the ego. You may think that you are acting loving, and yet loving is unconditionally understanding and accepting. Anything other than that is acting from the thoughts of the ego.

"Every time you look at your mate and want him or her to be different, or judge something about them, or are annoyed at what they are doing or how they are doing it, that is the ego trying to convince you that you are separate. Those thoughts keep you from remembering that the one in front of you is a Child of God, your brother and part of your Oneness. Without that one in front of you, your Oneness is not complete. You will need the one in front of you to attain your ultimate goal of Oneness even though you have forgotten it in this moment. Without that one in front of you, the puzzle is not complete and your Oneness will never be restored. You need the one in front of you and everyone behind them to be restored as Children of God, that the Oneness may be complete. At that time the ego will cease to exist. Just as your body's survival instinct is strong, so is the ego's. It will fight for its life. How it does that now is to continue to convince you of your separation."

Candace's Story

Candace: I grew up with a father who had been disillusioned by the Catholic Church after a strict Catholic upbringing, and with a mother who was agnostic. We didn't have a bible in our home, nor did my family go to church. On a few rare occasions, a neighbor took my sister and I to church, probably with the intention of saving us from our "heathen" parents. I thought Sunday School was interesting, but I knew that God wasn't waiting in a church for me to show up.

Despite my lack of religion, or maybe because of it, I had my own sense of God within me. I talked with God regularly, and I remember asking God and thanking God for things. Like many people, I had the common belief that God was in charge of my life and influenced what kind of day I had. If something went well, I thanked God. If something didn't go well, I blamed God. I also had the belief that I got what I deserved, so God was just doing what was fair.

After my parents divorced, I began praying, and the thing I prayed for the most was my family's safety. I would especially ask God to keep my mother safe since she was the person taking care of my sister and me. Over time I came to believe that if I didn't pray for my family, they wouldn't be safe. Soon, my prayers became more like pleading and begging, rather than asking, and I started to resent praying.

Over an eight year period, my misunderstandings and beliefs about who God was and how He impacted my life eventually became so painful that I gave up praying and stopped talking to God altogether. Then another eight years passed, during which I dropped out of high school, married and divorced my long time boyfriend, developed and overcame a drug problem, and graduated from college with a Bachelors in Social Work, ready to save the world, whatever that meant.

Around the time I was completing college, I stumbled upon a place called the Berkeley Psychic Institute (BPI). This was an organization that taught people how to use their psychic abilities. The belief at BPI was that everyone is spirit; therefore, their spiritual nature is their true essence. I liked this acknowledgment and felt very at home there. I learned meditation and energy healing techniques, and then joined their clairvoyant training program which focused on reading auras, chakras, past lives, etc. I enjoyed this 4th dimensional lifestyle tremendously, and I believed it gave me control over my reality.

When one graduated from BPI, they became a minister in the Church of Divine Man. There, God was called the "Supreme Being" and was perceived as a neutral entity. We were often instructed to connect to the Supreme Being or ask the Supreme Being for a healing. Our prayers were done as "mock ups." We would visualize what we wanted and then give that visualization to the Supreme Being to manifest for us. If you stayed grounded, which meant connected to the earth, your mock up would be granted. If you were ungrounded, which was very bad, your mock up wouldn't be granted.

One Christmas, I wasn't getting along with my family so I spent the day alone at the beach. I was sitting on top of a cliff looking out over the ocean, when suddenly I realized that Christmas was Jesus's birthday, so I said hello to Jesus within myself. Then I said, "Happy Birthday!" I asked Jesus what he would like for his birthday and his reply nearly made me fall off the cliff.

He said, "What I would like is for you to say 'hello' to people who cut you off on the road instead of calling them 'dickhead.'"

Other than maybe my best friend, no one knew that I called people dickhead on the road. I felt embarrassed and ashamed, even though there was no judgment in the communication.

Then Jesus said, "I will send people to cut you off so that they can get a special hello from you." It was the first time that I ever had a conversation with Jesus and I knew from the dickhead comment that I really was talking with him.

For many years thereafter, whenever someone cut me off on the road, I would remember that birthday request and honor it with a kind hello. When I did this, I was able to remember that the person in front of me wasn't a problem or a nuisance, but rather another human being sharing the same path with me, at least for that moment. I felt calmer and more peaceful, and I'm sure my driving improved.

One of the biggest concepts in BPI was separation and the idea that being totally separate from each other was the highest goal. We sought to have all of our own energy around us and no one else's energy anywhere near us. This concept made "love" a four letter word, because love involved blending energy. One of the most common phrases was, "You're in my space!" which meant that whatever problems I'm having are caused by your bad energy in my aura, chakras, the center of my head, and so on. We were also taught to erase other people's energy out of our space, with the belief that the energy we erased was gone forever.

Eventually, I began to think that this was not a lifestyle I wanted to continue. Around that time, my best friend gave me a book called *Mary's Message to the World*. The message I took from the book was that love was the pathway home to God, and returning to God was our true mission. That thought rang true in me and caused me to question all I had believed at BPI for the past 6 plus years. I was teaching meditation by then and I could no longer teach about separation, bad energy, and love being a four letter word. Needless to say, my days at BPI were numbered.

Shortly thereafter, I got into a car accident that allowed me to be off work for 9 weeks. This was a wonderful opportunity to assimilate all that I had been learning. During that time, a friend gave me a copy of a transcript by Jeshua (Jesus), as channeled through Jon Marc Hammer. In the transcript, Jeshua spoke of the world as something we dreamed up, rather than something real, and referred to our journey as one of remembering, rather than traveling. He said when we remember the Truth of who we are, we will realize we have never been separate from God and never could be. I devoured the Truth and inspiration in the message and I was changed forever just by reading it. My whole reality took on a new life, and my life took on a whole new reality.

The friend who gave me this transcript was a student at BPI. She also gave it to my friends, DavidPaul and Elif, and they too had similar experiences while reading it. We all spent that 9 week period together in what we called a "state of grace." A window into Reality had opened up for us and we could see that the world as we knew it was not real. We celebrated our new perspective every day and fell in love with life, each other, and whatever was in front of us. It was a deeply impacting time for all of us.

I enjoyed the transcript so much that I decided to get the book that Jon Marc Hammer had written, so I went to the bookstore. While I was there, I was pulled toward a big blue book on the shelf; that book was *A Course in Miracles* (ACIM). The man behind the counter told me that if I liked what Jon Marc Hammer had to say, I would definitely like *A Course in Miracles*. It was a book channeled by Jesus that teaches how to be restored to God. That was exactly what I wanted, so I took it home and began to read. I couldn't wrap my mind around the Text, so I started with the Workbook, which consisted of 365 lessons designed to be done one a day for a year. I could easily spend a month or more on each lesson, but I forced myself to keep moving because I was so hungry for what the Course had to say.

One beautiful January day, DavidPaul, Elif, and I went to Muir Woods to watch the sunrise before going to Stinson Beach for the day. While we were hiking, Elif suggested that we make up a song to commemorate our day. Not being in the habit of making up songs, I thought this would be a challenge. While we continued our hike, I opened my mouth and melodic words came out. I kept opening my mouth and more melodic words came out, followed by verses, until I had made up an entire song. The verses continued to come to me all day and I wrote some of them down. Here are a few of them:

The Sunrise Song

Oh we have traveled this long hard journey,
to get on home God, where we've always been.
We've always been there, we never left there;
we were just sleeping a long sound sleep.
Oh we are ready to go back home God;
we are ready to share your Love.
Take my hand God and hold it tightly;
take my hand and lead the way.
I'm not afraid God 'cuz you are with me,
and it is time to be the Light.
The Light You are that shines so brightly;
the Light inside of us, that Light we are.

Oh we have traveled this long hard journey,
to get on home where we've always been.

I was on a high that whole day without knowing that this was my first experience of bringing the Holy Spirit into the world.…

What is Right-Mindedness?

Candace: Holy Spirit, what is Right-Mindedness?

Holy Spirit: "The mind seems to be split and out of that split is the idea of Right-Mindedness, which is the Holy Spirit, and not Right-Mindedness, which is the ego. There is One Mind, just as there is Oneness, and it is a paradox to describe the fragmentation of this Mind because, in Truth, no one has ever nor could ever become separate from God or from the One Mind. At the same time, the power of the ego is strong enough to convince one otherwise. So even though it is not possible, there is the illusion or the dream that this has occurred. Within that 'reality,' which is not Reality in Truth, but one's given reality at present time, there is a 'Right-Mindedness' and a 'not Right-Mindedness,' and these are the two ways that the mind would think.

"If one is not in their Right-Mind, then they would hold the thoughts of the illusion of this world—fear, separation and death. This includes so many things: the idea that something or someone is better than another, that one is more valuable, that one wishes they could be the most important, all of the ideas of competition, success, striving, gratification, addictions, and these types of things. These thoughts exist when one is out of their Right-Mind and they are pursuing distractions and illusions. They are chasing the carrot that they will never catch. This is the perfect image to describe the world—everyone is chasing a carrot on a string in front of them that they will never catch, and that is the good news. What the world has to offer, you would not want. Never catching that carrot is a blessing.

"Right-Mindedness is the Holy Spirit's thinking. It is a way of correcting your perceptions so that you are able to see yourself and the one in front of you as a Child of God. You are able to see the Truth of a situation or to understand that there has never been attack or mistake or sin. This is not One-Mindedness, but it is part of the journey to One-Mindedness.

"Each time you restore your mind to Right-Mindedness, you reclaim a little piece of that part of your mind for yourself and it is harder for the ego to infiltrate that area in the future, if there were such a thing. Each time you choose Right-

Mindedness, each time you choose to see the Truth in a situation, you reclaim a little of your sanity for yourself. Eventually this does build and grow into a significant piece that allows you to have much more command over choosing Right-Mindedness in any given moment. You begin to know that what you are thinking, seeing, and perceiving is, in fact, insane and you would like to see differently. You stop for a moment and you connect with your Right-Mind, in whatever way each one does that, and you restore yourself to sanity.

"Eventually, as your mind is restored over time and this restoration builds and builds, one day what you have is Right-Mindedness. Right-Mindedness is the cure to ego. It is the correction of the ego's thinking; therefore, it must acknowledge and understand the ego in some way to be the cure. This is what will lead you into One-Mindedness, so that you never again are capable of thinking a thought about the ego or from the ego. In One-Mindedness, it is no longer possible to think like the ego. God cannot think the thoughts of the ego. God does not even perceive the ego because One-Mindedness is not capable of doing that.

"It is easy to perceive the ego as the enemy and think that you are now perceiving with Right-Mindedness. It is important to remember that you made the ego because you wanted to have a certain experience. You wanted your autonomy, just as a teenager or young adult might decide that they are ready to leave home and be on their own and they want the opportunity to try. This is what this aspect of God has done as well. They are not wrong for wanting that. They are not wrong in how they go about it. They are all learning experiences. Each one does the best they can to survive in the world. It is the same with these aspects of God. You made this tool, and it has done exactly what you asked of it. If you perceive the ego as the enemy, you have lost and the ego has won. Your ultimate goal is to not perceive the ego. That does not mean you ignore it or deny it or pretend it does not exist. That is not the case at all. It is just that not perceiving the ego is the ultimate goal, and that will come with One-Mindedness and it will not come before then.

"The more that one hears God, the less they hear the ego. It is just that simple. The less that one hears God, the more they hear the ego. So if you are hearing God's Voice, you are turning down the volume on the ego. They cannot talk over each other. In Truth, the Holy Spirit cannot talk over the ego. The ego may be rambling in your mind, and you will have to stop and say, 'I do not want to perceive in this way,' or 'I want to perceive Truth now,' or 'This hurts. I don't want this pain anymore.' There has to be a moment where you stop the rambling of the ego and you choose differently, and in that moment, you invite the Holy Spirit to speak.

"The Holy Spirit will not speak over the ego, though it will happily speak in place of the ego. The more that you choose to hear God's Voice, the less opportunity the ego has to speak, until one day you are engaged with the Holy Spirit when you wake up and throughout the day and when you go to sleep. That is where you have your awareness and that is what serves your thinking, your mind, your life, and your actions. You are focused on that which truly serves you, that which brings you peace.

"Ultimately, this continual joining with the Holy Spirit offers you peace. You start to notice that peace becomes a way of life. It does not matter if there are wars, bombs, or killings going on right outside your door or in your own home. What you notice is that all you have is peace within you, and it becomes obvious when that peace is threatened. You immediately notice that threat rather than living with it for years.

"The more that you have peace, the more easily recognizable it is when you do not. You are able to quickly remind yourself that in fact you would like to be restored to Right-Mindedness. Then you breathe. Then you go to the Holy Spirit. You feel, hear, or know that connection and you breathe again. And you go about your day with your peace restored, going longer and longer periods in peace and truly, ultimately, one day, that will be all you know. That could be today or any other day you choose.

"Do not have fear that you shouldn't bother focusing on it now because it is light years into the future. There is no such thing as time or space. No time has ever transpired from the instant you had the thought that you were separate from God. You had that thought and then that thought will fall away and you will be restored to God, and it will be that long that you perceived that you were not with God, though in fact you never were separate.

"You and the ego invented time and space to prove these theories of separation, but there is no time and no space. Start now choosing to restore your mind to Right-Mindedness, to Sanity, to Truth, and know that each time you do that, it builds on itself to the point that you will no longer be able to choose hearing the ego. It will not be a viable choice, not because the ego is an enemy but because what it has to offer, you no longer see as more valuable than peace. The ego has served its purpose and now you choose peace.

"When you think upon the ego and you become afraid, threatened or angry, you can stop for a moment and bless the ego and thank it for all the ways that it served you. You can say, 'Until next time,' and close that door and open the one to the Holy Spirit. When you do this, you give yourself the gift of the kind of experience, encounter, or interaction you want to have with the ego when you do think of it. If you think of the ego and become afraid, that is the ego-mind work-ing. If you become aware of the ego and you bless it and allow it to be, and you close the door and choose differently, then you are in Right-Mindedness. To try to never think of the ego again or to be threatened by the thought that you might think of the ego, *is* the ego. Give yourself the gift of peace in your thinking about the ego and then you know you are thinking with the Holy Spirit. There is noth-ing to fear but a thought and you can always think differently.

"Part of the magic of the Holy Spirit is that the more you share the Holy Spirit, the more you have of the Holy Spirit. The more that you give It away, the more that you acknowledge It in another, the more that you choose the Holy Spirit's thinking, and the more that you acknowledge the Holy Spirit in yourself, the more *you* have the Holy Spirit. That which is eternal gains by sharing it.

"Eventually, you will turn more and more of your painful thinking over to the Holy Spirit and ask for restoration. You will have more and more thoughts of Truth, and there will come a time when, in fact, you will hear the Holy Spirit so consistently and so frequently that the ego will not have the opportunity to inter-rupt and jump in, or when you notice the ego interrupting and jumping in, it will be so obvious, so distinctly different than what you have become used to, that you will immediately be able to restore your mind to the Holy Spirit. The ego does not go away; it just becomes quiet. It is only a rambling voice in the back of your mind, so if it is quiet, it has no other power."

What is Forgiveness?

Candace: Holy Spirit, what is forgiveness?

Holy Spirit: "Forgiveness is the path of the Holy Spirit. The Holy Spirit uses forgiveness to correct perceptions and perceive Truth. The Truth of any situation is that no sin has occurred, no error accomplished, no Brother has wronged. The Truth is that the one in front of you, along with yourself, is only Perfection and cannot be, never has been, nor ever will be anything other than Perfection. When the ego begins to perceive something other than the Truth, forgiveness is the opportunity to overlook this misperception. To 'overlook' means to look beyond what you are perceiving—look over it, past it, beyond it and see the Truth, the Truth that God's Child has never done anything wrong. As you overlook the ego's perceptions, you use the Holy Spirit's thinking to go straight to the Truth.

"Forgiveness is the means to quiet the ego, in the sense that when one misper-ceives and believes what they misperceive, they are believing the ego in that moment. When one looks past that with forgiveness and with the Holy Spirit and sees only the Truth, they are not validating the ego or giving the ego power. They are instead quieting the ego. Forgiveness is the gift you give yourself of experiencing Truth in any situation, thereby having peace.

"Believing that forgiveness is necessary can also be a concept of the ego, and yet forgiveness is the opportunity to correct your thinking; therefore, it *is* the Holy Spirit's thinking and is used to restore you to the Truth. Though forgiveness couldn't be necessary or possible when one is *only* perceiving Truth, while one is perceiving with both the ego and the Holy Spirit, forgiveness is the path away from the ego—and to God.

"Used in its highest form or for its highest purpose, forgiveness has the potential to offer you peace and right-mindedness. When used for the ego's purposes, it can continue to take you deeper and deeper into misperceptions. One may attempt to prove the misperceptions, clarify the misperceptions, understand the misperceptions, believe the misperceptions, and then forgive the misperceptions for the sake of the other, rather than for their own peace. When used by the Holy Spirit, it is the pathway to peace.

"When one overlooks sin, error, or misperception, they overlook it in themselves as well as in the one in front of them. All is forgiven and only Christ is experienced. To remember the Truth of Who and What God's Child is gives you the experience of being God's Child. Because that is all you have ever been or ever will be, that is where your true peace lies."

Chapter Highlights

"The Holy Spirit's function and purpose is to bring God's Voice to each of God's children, guiding them, directing them, loving them, and restoring their thinking to Right-Mindedness and Truth."

"If you think of the ego and become afraid, that is the ego-mind working. If you become aware of the ego and you bless it and allow it to be, and you close the door and choose differently, then you are in Right-Mindedness."

"Though forgiveness couldn't be necessary or possible when one is *only* perceiving Truth, while one is perceiving with both the ego and the Holy Spirit, forgiveness is the path away from the ego—and to God."

2

The Son

"God's Love is the Source of who you are.
God's Love cannot change,
and neither can you."

Holy Spirit: "God's Child, God's holy, beloved Child is so cherished and so loved that It is allowed to perceive Itself in any way It desires. It is allowed to experience Itself as anything, even something other than a beloved and cherished and holy Child of God. There is a saying in the world 'There, but for the grace of God, go I.' In reality, it is 'There, but for the perception of the ego, go I.' When one perceives themselves as separate and different than the one in front of them, they can only be looking through the eyes of the ego. When one perceives the one in front of them as themselves, when one no longer looks with the eyes of the ego but looks instead with the Sight of the Holy Spirit, they are able to see the Truth of who and what they are."

DavidPaul's Story

DavidPaul: When I left the Air Force Academy in the summer of 1989, I plunged headlong into a spiritual path. I didn't know what I was looking for, but I read anything I could get my hands on—*Illusions*, *Autobiography of Yogi*, *A Bridge Across Forever*, the *Tao Te Ching*, the *Bhagavad Gita*, *The Way of the Peaceful Warrior*—whatever I could find to deepen my understanding of life and who I was.

17

That fall, I applied to UC Berkeley as a transfer student. To my surprise, they rejected me, though they had previously accepted my application as a high school senior. I had excellent grades at the Academy, lived in Moscow for nine months…. It just didn't make sense. I was furious. So I re-applied, and again they rejected me.

I had only applied to two schools, UC Berkeley and UC Santa Barbara. I was accepted at UC Santa Barbara, but I wanted to go to UC Berkeley and I wasn't going to give up. I petitioned, wrote letters, introduced myself to professors, and did everything I could think of to counter their decision. In all, I received five separate rejection letters. Not willing to accept defeat, I petitioned one last time, and for whatever reason, I was accepted.

It was during my first semester at Cal that my mother suddenly passed away. She had become very sick, had a stroke while walking across the street, and was gone before I knew it. I hadn't seen or spoken to her for months when I received the phone call from the hospital.

Looking back, her death was a great gift to me. Although it had only been a year since my revelation listening to Kenny G, I was already beginning to fall back into worldly ambitions at Berkeley. So when the semester ended a few weeks after my mother passed away, I packed my camping gear, hitchhiked to Yosemite, and backpacked deep into the mountains where I lived in a cave and meditated from morning till night. It was there that I tasted for the first time in my life, the peace and joy that comes from going within.

When I came down from the mountain three weeks later, I was at peace with my mother's death and my experience of life was no longer the same. My interest in school or a successful career had vanished, and all I could think about was going within, searching for Truth, and trying to figure out my purpose in life.

When I returned to school that fall, I hardly attended my classes. Instead, I spent most of my time reading spiritual books and studying Tai Chi. Through a friend of mine, I fell into a job being a "house brother" at a sorority, receiving free room and board in exchange for watching over the house. When I finally graduated from school the following spring, I had no motivation to get a real job or start a career, so I kept my job at the sorority house.

With nothing but free time over the summer, I signed up for a meditation class at the Berkeley Psychic Institute. Within a couple of weeks, I was hooked. I registered for every class they offered, including their year-long clairvoyant training program. It was there at the Institute that I first met Candace.

The Berkeley Psychic Institute was a fascinating place. They taught a way of seeing the world unlike anything I had ever experienced. With my cushy job at the sorority house, I spent eight hours a day at the Institute giving psychic readings for nearly two years. Over that time, Candace and I became close friends. Then one day, someone handed us a channeled transcript from Jesus.

On the second page of the transcript, Jesus said, "Sin means simply to have missed the mark, to have forgotten the Truth of your being. Never once—and I know this may sound a bit radical—never once did I come into this plane to tell you that you need a savior to save you from your sins. It is not truth that I shed my blood for the salvation of many. I came with but one simple Gospel, and, unto anyone who would listen, I would look into their eyes and say but one thing: 'you are already the one you seek. And that which you would strive to be forgiven for has already been forgiven. And the past that has weighed you down already has been destroyed by the Light of the perfect Love that this world cannot comprehend.'

"Now, I'm very sorry but I cannot come forth and give unto you forty-three years of complex techniques that if you but master them, then you might be worthy to get it. I will leave that up to many that come unto you and love to keep you guessing. And I will leave it up to those of you who insist on forty-three more years of complex struggle so you can enjoy your drama. And yet, you must in the end come to where you are even in this moment. For it is the only place that you can remember the Truth of the Kingdom: to look not with the eyes that are born of your world, but to look through the eyes of the awakened Christ....

"For many would teach you that you can create your own reality. Yet, I say unto you: your reality is one, and it is simple and it is given to you freely since before time is. You have never lost it. You have only forgotten."

In the moment that I read those words, something miraculous happened. I *experienced* the Truth of who I am for the first time in my life, and when I did, everything that I had ever believed instantly fell away. I no longer believed any of it—what I had learned at the Institute, in all my years of schooling, or in my life—none of it. I knew that all of it was just a belief, just a thought, and had absolutely no impact on the Truth of who I am.

It was probably the most powerful experience of my life. Never before and never since has so much fallen away in a single moment. To some, this might sound frightening, but it wasn't. It was the most liberating, most joyful, most profound experience of my life....

Who is God's Child?

DavidPaul: Holy Spirit, can you explain who we are in relationship to God?

Holy Spirit: "God, in all of His Love, extended that Love, which then became God's Child. God and His Child have played together, loved together, laughed together, and that has never changed. Then God's Child had the thought that it could be separate from its Father and there was a split in the mind that then caused that Child to think it was separate. The Child then made the ego to reinforce the separation, which then fabricated the world, which allowed for a place for separation to occur.

"One cannot be separate from something if there is nowhere else to go, so the world was invented out of the need to go somewhere that God could not. It is literally like stepping into a painting on the wall and imagining now that you live in that painting and you are running in the fields and smelling the flowers and looking at the water when, in fact, you have merely projected yourself into that painting and are imagining yourself moving about in it. In Reality, you are not in that piece of canvas on the wall, just as God's Child has not left God's Lap.

"When the ego and the world were made, the Father created the Holy Spirit as a gift to the Child to find its way out of that canvas. As the Child entered the world, it perceived itself in fragments, in separate pieces, and as more and more of it entered into the world, more and more pieces of it seemed to enter as well. Now it appears there are more than six billion pieces of itself roaming around that canvas, interacting with different parts of it, taking on different roles within it, having a wide variety of experiences while there, and yet it is just this one projection of the Child that appears to be in all of these pieces.

"Little by little, these pieces will return to the One. The first piece to do this perfectly was the one who was known as Jesus. He came into the world, fulfilled his function of remembering the Truth of who and what he is, and restored himself back to the One Child; however, those six billion fragments are still in need of returning, which is only a thought away.

"In the world, one can be referred to as a Child of God. This is true, and yet there is only One Child of God. As you look around in the world and you see ones who you perceive as good and bad, mean or kind, smart or not, and so on, you are looking at God's Child through the eyes of the ego and no Child of God is available to you with this perspective.

"When you look with the Vision of the Holy Spirit, all you see is yourself in front of you, next to you, across from you, everywhere you look, and you recognize that, in fact, you are in a hall of mirrors and that all around you is you. In some mirrors you look tall, in some you look short, in some you look fat, in some you look wiggly, and so on, and yet it is all you in every mirror you look in. In fact, there is only One. It just appears differently in this fragmented and distorted place.

"As you step out of the hall of mirrors and you look around, there is only One. That is all the world is—a hall of mirrors. You have been imagining yourself there, when in fact you never were. And as each fragment returns Home to Itself, that is what is ultimately referred to as the Child of God, the Oneness, the Sonship. The ego takes you deeper into the hall of mirrors, and the Holy Spirit will guide you out.

"Part of your responsibility to yourself is to take with you any other parts of you that you find in that hall of mirrors that are willing and ready to go. You do that by recognizing in a perceived other, in one that you perceive as other than you, that in Truth, they are you, that you are not separate, that the one you imagine in front of you is, in Truth, God's only beloved Child. You remind that one in front of you of the Truth of who they are and you do that by being certain of who you are and you take them with you. God's Child is everywhere you look, everyone you see, everyone you like and don't like, love and don't love. When you give yourself the gift of recognizing the Truth of who you are and the Truth of who another is, it is the richest experience you can have in the world."

Who was Jesus?

DavidPaul: Holy Spirit, who was Jesus when he walked upon the earth and what was his relationship to the Holy Spirit?

Holy Spirit: "At the time that you had the thought that you wanted your autonomy and you made the ego while God simultaneously created the Holy Spirit, there was the understanding that this was a temporary experiment and that it would have an end. That end would be when all of God's children were restored to God. Eventually, there came a time when someone stepped into the world with the hope, the dream, and the goal of hearing only the Holy Spirit and not hearing anything else. That person was Jesus.

"Jesus has been referred to as God's Son and yet every person in the world is God's Son. There is no distinction there. The only difference between Jesus and you is the desire, commitment, and follow through to hear only the Holy Spirit and to not engage with the ego. This did not happen instantaneously, spontaneously, or at birth. It happened over time, as you know it in the world, with practice and dedication and the desire to think only Truth, to speak only Truth, and to hear only Truth. As a result of this desire and commitment, Jesus came to hear only the Holy Spirit and came to speak only the Words of the Holy Spirit.

"If you want to know how the Holy Spirit sounds or what Right-Mindedness is, it is the Words that Jesus spoke in the world. When Jesus shared certain truths, perspectives, and Right-Mindedness, this came directly from the Holy Spirit. Jesus could have kept those thoughts to himself and not shared them, and yet what would be the point of that?

"It is important to note how many wanted to hear Jesus speak. People would flock to hear what he had to say. Many years after his death, people wrote down what they remember he said, and for two thousand years afterward, people continue to read those Words. The power of those Words comes from the Truth being brought into the world through the Voice of God, the Holy Spirit, as spoken to Jesus. Jesus's body was used as a tool for communication and served no other purpose—that is how the Holy Spirit would use the body.

"Everyone desires to hear the Truth because that is what they are. They have nearly forgotten, and yet they desire that reminder completely. When one brings the Words of the Holy Spirit into the world, many will flock to hear them. One cannot help but want to hear Truth. It is a part of you. The same Holy Spirit exists within every child, with the same message to deliver, and every child wants that message. The staying power that Jesus has in the world comes from a single-mindedness, the single focus upon Truth and conveying only Truth. That is very attractive indeed. Jesus has not swayed for an instant since then and continues to hold only Right-Mindedness and continues to be joined in perfect clarity with the Holy Spirit. He has overcome perception altogether, so all that is left is knowledge.

"One often asks, 'How can I maintain this perception of Right-Mindedness?' It would be a challenge indeed to try to fight for that perception of Reality throughout eternity. When one hears the Holy Spirit more and more and the ego less and less until finally only the Holy Spirit is heard, eventually or as an outcome of that, truly the split in the mind that was the ego is gone. It was never real to begin with and once Reality has taken hold of the mind, all that is not real falls away. That is when True Knowledge exists rather than perception.

"Jesus has True Knowledge, not a perception of Truth, and is able to maintain that Knowledge completely and perfectly for all of eternity because that is all there is. There is no fight to attain and maintain that Knowledge. It becomes effortless because it is all there is. Jesus does not have to question or wonder about the Truth of who you are, ever, regardless of your belief that you are something other than a Child of God. Jesus does not have to waste a thought wondering if you might be right about that. He has only perfect Knowledge.

"As a Child of God, having walked in the world in a body, there is the ability for Jesus to understand his brothers and sisters in the world and why they think the way they do, and just like the Holy Spirit, he does not believe what they think. One can therefore use Jesus in the same way as the Holy Spirit—one can ask Jesus to work with their mind to be restored to Right-Mindedness. Jesus will deny you nothing, though you must ask for it. Jesus's function is to nudge his brothers and sisters out of their sleep and to assist them in whatever ways possible in their awakening, and He does this by only seeing their Perfection.

"Jesus eventually became the embodiment of the Holy Spirit and you will too. It is only a matter of time, and the wonderful news is, there is no such thing as time. So in an instant, having remembered the Truth of who you are and where you have come from, you too will be the embodiment of the Holy Spirit, taking your rightful place with God and Jesus."

Is There Truth in the Bible?

DavidPaul: There are many who believe that the Bible is the Word of God, and yet so much of what you've said contradicts the Bible. How can you explain that?

Holy Spirit: "While there is some Truth in the Bible, there is non-Truth as well. There is no way to prove what is true while living in the world. However, with the understanding that the world is just a dream, then what has occurred within the world is a dream as well. What has been written that is called history comes from the perspective of a few and has been changed over time to reflect different points of view and different agendas.

"God did not create the world. God does not live in the world, and God does not influence the world. As such, most of what one might read in the Bible does not appear to be true. It is not God's Will that there be sin, punishment, guilt, or suffering. The only way that one can know what is true for them is to go within and ask. When you hear God's Voice within you and receive the guidance, the love, the compassion, the forgiveness, and the acceptance that God's Voice has for you, you will know what is true.

"What parent wants their child to suffer? What parent wants their child to believe that they will only be loved by their parent if they do certain things or do not do other things? Parents want their children to know that they are loved no matter what, that they are safe and secure and loved and cared for in every moment.

"If that is your belief about God, you may not find much of that God in the Bible, but you will find that within you. Let the Holy Spirit be your Bible. Trust only what you know to be God's Voice to guide and direct you, to serve and influence you, so that you may always know that you are loved and safe and cared for no matter what."

Chapter Highlights

"When you look with the Vision of the Holy Spirit, all you see is yourself in front of you, next to you, across from you, everywhere you look, and you recognize that, in fact, you are in a hall of mirrors and that all around you is you."

"Jesus has been referred to as God's Son and yet every person in the world is God's Son. There is no distinction there. The only difference between Jesus and you is the desire, commitment, and follow through to hear only the Holy Spirit and to not engage with the ego."

"The only way that one can know what is true for them is to go within and ask. When you hear God's Voice within you and receive the guidance, the love, the compassion, the forgiveness, and the acceptance that God's Voice has for you, you will know what is true."

3

The World

"God's Love is given to me,
unending, unchanged, and unconditional,
and only a thought keeps me from it."

Holy Spirit: "The world was made once upon a time, and within that time, there is life and death, joy and pain, suffering and pleasure, though in Reality, none of those things exist. They are just part of a long dream that is the world. In that dream, anything can happen, though when one finally wakes up, they recognize that it has just been a dream, that none of it was real, and that everything is as it was created."

DavidPaul's Story Continued

DavidPaul: Only days after our life changing experience reading the Jeshua transcript, Candace and I discovered *A Course in Miracles*. It beautifully echoed our newfound experience of the world and quickly became our guide. Several weeks later, we went to Stinson Beach to celebrate. We spent the day enjoying the sunshine, playing Frisbee, and splashing around at the water's edge. There, Candace told me that a lifelong dream of hers had been to swim in the ocean. Having grown up in California, she had always been frustrated with the temperature of the water. I too had always loved the ocean and wanted to live in a place where I could comfortably enjoy it.

While playing, our Frisbee accidentally landed on a man lying in the sun. When we went to retrieve it, he told us that his name was Matisha, and he asked if he could join us. We noticed that he had *A Course in Miracles* with him, and we asked him about it. He told us he taught the principles of the Course in prisons and that he was on his way to Hawaii to do some teaching there as well. He said that he spent every winter in Hawaii, swimming in the ocean, connecting with dolphins, and enjoying the warmth and sunshine. As he spoke, our eyes lit up! Candace and I turned to one another at the same moment and smiled from ear to ear. Somehow, we just knew we were moving to Hawaii.

The following weeks were a whirlwind—saying goodbye to friends and family, quitting my job, leaving the Institute, getting rid of my belongings. Before I knew it, I was stepping off the plane on Kauai carrying only a backpack and two books, *A Course in Miracles* and *The Way of the Servant*.

The day I arrived, a terrible rainstorm struck the island. It rained buckets for nearly two weeks. Tired of sleeping in a wet tent, I rented a studio apartment on the North Shore. Two days later, I fell into a part-time job at the Princeville Hotel. By the time Candace arrived a week later, I had unexpectedly begun a life on Kauai. Looking back on it, it seems funny that we never ended up living on the same island together, but it honestly never occurred to either of us to turn our friendship into something more. After staying with me for a week, Candace continued onward to the Big Island where she settled down.

I stepped off the plane in Hawaii overflowing with life. I had never felt so incredibly free. For a number of months, I *was* the Second Coming. I knew the Truth, and nothing could take it from me. I even stopped reading the Course. I thought, "I don't need to read about the Truth. I'm living It."

But as the months slowly passed, the light and life within me began to grow dimmer and dimmer. I was still absolutely certain of the Truth I had experienced only months before, but no matter how certain I was of its Reality, I did not have the understanding or experience to apply this Truth to my life as I walked in the illusion of the world. As a result, I slowly began to disconnect from the world one thought at a time.

Not really knowing what I was doing, I watched my thoughts like a hawk. As each thought would arise within me, I would swiftly strike it down. I was a thought destroying machine and proud of it. Nothing was going to take me away from living the Truth of who I am again...but I was mistaken.

As a result of judging every thought that arose within me, it didn't take long for the joy and passion I once had to drain from my life. With each passing day, I grew more and more disconnected. Not understanding that I was literally rejecting the world and everything in it by trying to eliminate my thoughts in this way, I soon found myself meditating from morning till night because it was the only place in my life where I could find any real peace or joy. It was the only place in my life where I could truly silence my thoughts and lay down my sword.

After many months of sitting in silence, unable to find or acknowledge any value in the world, I summoned my determination to be done with this meaningless game once and for all. If meditation was the only place I could find peace, I had to take it to the end. I couldn't take the life I had made any longer. So I went to a deserted beach one day, sat down beneath a tall tree, and vowed to remain there until I became enlightened. It was the only way out, or so I thought.

I meditated under the tree for nearly 10 hours straight. As the sun dipped below the horizon that evening, a deep realization sunk in—no matter how badly I wanted to escape the lifeless world I was living in, I wasn't going to will myself out of it and into enlightenment. And even if it were possible, I just knew it wasn't going to happen for me. So I opened my eyes, got up, and walked myself home.

This humbling experience ultimately became a tremendous turning point for me in learning how to live a life filled with Truth while still walking in the illusion of the world....

What is the World?

DavidPaul: Holy Spirit, what is the world and who created it?

Holy Spirit: "At the time that God's Child made the ego, the ego then fabricated the world as a way to assist in your autonomy. If you live in a place where God cannot go, then your autonomy is assured. God does not go into the world because the world does not exist. There is nothing for God to go into. You believe in the world and that is how the world has come to be, but God does not. The world is a thought that you made, along with the ego that you made, to serve your desire for autonomy. It has only ever been a thought, is only now a thought, and will only ever be a thought.

"There are more than 6 billion of God's Children who hold the same thought. They may perceive the world a little differently—each one does—but each one has the belief that the world is real and that taking a body and stepping onto this merry-go-round that is the world is an adventure and comes with rules, goals, and aspirations. Those are all thoughts that you made. God did not create the world. God did not create the earth. God did not create bodies or anything else upon the earth. God did not create the goals or the rules or anything of the world.

"As a loving parent, God does not stop His Children from thinking what they want to think. He merely loves them and waits patiently for them to think differently so that they can be rejoined with their Father completely. The world and everything in it has only the value that you give it. It has only the meaning you attach to it and the purpose you assign it. The world has no meaning for God, though God honors your need for healing your mind in the sense of recognizing that, in fact, you are not and cannot be separate from God.

"God did not create bodies. If one lives or dies, is healed or not, is maimed or not, that has nothing to do with God. It has only to do with one's thinking. Within the illusion of the world, the Holy Spirit uses bodies as a means of communication. That is their sole purpose. Of themselves, they have no other value. If a plant or an animal lives or dies, that has nothing to do with God. If the earth becomes poisoned to the point of its demise, that has nothing to do with God. God did not create it. God cannot and will not save it. It does not exist in Reality, so what is there to save?

"One's worldly goals have nothing to do with Truth or God. If one pursues a degree, a position, a business, a home, a family, or anything else of the world, that has nothing to do with God and everything to do with the world, the beliefs in the world, and the need to prove autonomy. They have nothing to do with Reality or God. God created you, and as a creation of God, you are an extension of God. You couldn't be anything but Perfection. When you think of yourself as anything but Perfection, you cannot help but think of God as something imperfect. You are then implying God's imperfection by your own thoughts of imperfection. Because you are an extension of God, your will is an extension of God's Will. Therefore, your will and God's Will are one and the same.

"The world is an opportunity to be distracted away from God. One could look at a butterfly or a sunrise or a rainbow and have the thought, 'There is God' or 'God must be real' or 'God made that.' In truth, those are all distractions away from God. The ego keeps you focused on a butterfly or a sunrise or a rainbow rather than the Truth. It is not to say that there should be no regard for life, but rather to say that what exists in the world, in Truth, has not been created by God. And in Reality, life or death does not exist in the physical sense. There is only life everlasting, in the sense of God's Child and in your relationship to God, and that cannot change.

"You *can* allow the world to serve you while you are in it so that when you have the thought 'God must be real' or 'God must have made that' you can stop and truly focus on God instead of on that sunrise, so that you use it as a reminder rather than a distraction. You can stop and connect with God, connect with the Holy Spirit, connect with Yourself, and reaffirm your Oneness, your desire to hear God's Voice, to know the Truth, and to value what is truly of value, not that which you have come to believe is valuable.

"Use the world as a playground to heal and awaken yourself and your brothers and sisters rather than as a place to take seriously, to be burdened by, to fight against, to be disappointed in, or to wish were different. Allow it to be a place where your brothers and sisters are awakening with you. You can join them in getting up, stretching, yawning, and coming alive with Truth. You can join them in your heart and mind and then go out into the world to tap another on the shoulder, giving them a gentle nudge to awaken them. If they fall back to sleep, let them rest a while and then move to another, nudging them gently and lovingly. Allow the world to be a place that heals. Allow it to serve you and allow what you see in the world to be gentle reminders of Truth."

What is the Earth?

DavidPaul: In saying that the world is only an illusion, how do plants and animals and the Earth fit into this?

Holy Spirit: "If all that exists is God, God's Child, and God's Voice, then the world and everything in the world is an illusion. They are a part of the dream—the dream of separation. If everything in the world is an illusion, this would include plants, animals, trees, insects, ocean life, and anything else that appears to be alive. In Truth, none of these things exist. They are projected out of a thought from the split mind to again prove that separation is real. They do not exist, never have, and never will. They are just a part of the vivid imagination of the ego that serves as a distraction from Truth."

DavidPaul: What about when I'm talking to God? Is that an illusion too? Does God even know when I'm talking to him?

Holy Spirit: "If the world is not real and all that goes on in the world then is not real, and if God does not enter the world that is not real, God knows not what happens in the world. When one has a conversation with God, when one acknowledges God, appreciates God, gives thanks to God, expresses love in whatever ways they do, God hears every word. God acknowledges every loving thought, every kind intention.

"When one sleepwalks about in the world ranting and raving at God, scolding God, threatening God, and so on, God does not hear any of that because it is not His Child speaking to Him. When one is yelling at God, it is the ego that is angry; it is the ego that is yelling. Because the ego isn't real and God does not acknowledge what is not real, God cannot hear what is not real.

"The angry thoughts—the ranting, raving, and threats—have never been received or heard by God. Therefore, there is no need for one to feel guilty or ashamed or embarrassed by these words or thoughts. It was not *You* who said them or thought them. It was not God who received them. That is how the ego thinks, how the ego perceives, how the ego reacts. It is really only the ego that hears and acknowledges its own ranting and raving. It is the ego that feels shame and guilt. It is the ego that is angry.

"Given that, all that is left is forgiveness and peace, knowing that your relationship with God is completely intact, as it always has been and always will be, regardless of what you might think you may have thought or said or done."

Exercise—Playing in the World of Truth

Holy Spirit: "It is easy to hear that God did not create the world and then think that the world has no meaning for you, or to hear that God is not in the world, therefore, the world must not have any value. The world is what you made, and it can be used, with the help of the Holy Spirit, to either assist you in falling deeper into your sleep or it can assist you in waking up.

"Take some time to walk about in the world—whether that is in your home, outdoors, at your work, wherever it may be—and as you walk, notice what you notice. Do not try to notice something, but allow something to become known to you. And imagine for yourself how what you notice could assist you in reminding you of the Truth of who you are and/or reminding you of the Truth of God.

"Everything that you made has the potential to either take you further away or bring you closer to the Truth, depending on your perspective. The ego's perspective will take you away, and the Holy Spirit's perspective will bring you to the Truth. In allowing yourself to focus on something and becoming aware of how it can assist you in remembering the Truth of who you are and the Truth of God, you can allow the world to serve you in the most amazing ways and ultimately quicken your journey Home. You may want to spend a few minutes or longer every day practicing moving about in the world with this intention and noticing how everything has the possibility to serve you with the right state of mind.

"For example, when you pay for something at a store, pull money out of your pocket, or find a coin on the street, you can have the thought that money is the root of all evil. You can have the thought that you never have enough money. You can have the thought that things are too expensive…. Or you can have the thought that you have this resource to get what you need and that, for the most part, you always have had it and always will. Or you can stop for a moment and thank God, thank the Holy Spirit, or thank yourself for always having what you need in the world, knowing and trusting that that will always be the case. You can also go beyond that and have the money be a symbol to you that you always have what you *truly* want and need, which is God, God's Love, and God's Voice. In terms of Right-Mindedness, you can go as far as you want. Right-Mindedness can be a small shift into a positive perspective or a deeper shift into a place of gratitude or connection with the Holy Spirit…possibly transcending the world and allowing something to directly link you back to your connection with God.

"It can be the same for a dead animal in the road. One might think, 'Oh, that is awful," or 'I hate death,' or something about the person who hit the animal or the animal itself…. Or one might stop and give thanks for having had that animal in the world. One might take a moment to trust that it must be perfect…. 'This animal's life must be complete. It must have fulfilled its purpose.' Or you can go further and take a moment to connect with God…to remember and to trust that, in Reality, there is no death. Spirit cannot be killed. The body is temporary, transitory, and illusory, and that the essence of whatever it is that appears to have died has never changed and will never change.

"Everything in the world, with a certain perspective and a certain intention, can be used to bring you closer to the Truth. It is only to stop for a moment and to notice your thoughts, which more naturally gravitate toward the struggles of the world, and to acknowledge them, thank the ego for doing its job, and to search within your heart and mind for that which is really True, for that which gives you Peace or Joy or Comfort, because everything in the world can serve you in that way if you allow it."

Chapter Highlights

"Use the world as a playground to heal and awaken yourself and your brothers and sisters rather than as a place to take seriously, to be burdened by, to fight against, to be disappointed in, or to wish were different. Allow it to serve you and allow what you see in the world to be gentle reminders of Truth."

"Everything that you made has the potential to either take you further away or bring you closer to the Truth, depending on your perspective. The ego's perspective will take you away, and the Holy Spirit's perspective will bring you to the Truth."

4

The Father

"God knows only Perfect Love.
God sees only Perfect Love.
God is only Perfect Love."

Holy Spirit: "God is the All Loving, All Knowing Creator of what is. God's Love knows no bounds. God's Love is limitless and enduring, and God has nothing but Love to be, to share, and to do. God's Love is all there is, all there ever has been, and all there ever will be. When one sees something other than God's Love, they are just mis-seeing. It is not possible for there to be anything else. When you see anything other than God's Love, you can shake your head and look again knowing that you must be mistaken. God's Love is the source of all that is. When one looks through the eyes of Truth, that will be all they see."

Who is God?

Candace: Holy Spirit, because our beliefs about God impact us in so many ways, can you explain Who God is?

Holy Spirit: "It is easy to say that God is all there is. To understand this, you would have to understand the distinction between what is Real and what is imagined, what God created and what you dreamed. In Reality, God is all there is and only God and what God created exist—God, God's Child, and the Holy Spirit are what exist, and God's Child and the Holy Spirit exist within God.

"God just is, and God can only be what you project on to Him to be. The beliefs of God being love or peace or truth are worldly concepts. It's the highest attainable in the world, and yet once you step out of the illusion of the world, you see that those are not what is the most attainable for God. God just is. There are no stories, no concepts of good or bad, right or wrong, peace or not peace, love or not love. God just is, without any expectations, without any demands, without any judgments. The highest concept of what that might look like in the world is unconditional Love.

"God is unconditionally loving because God is nothing else. God is only capable of seeing you as Perfection. You are not capable of being anything other than Perfection, except in your own mind. Because God loves you the way He does, you are free to pursue your own dreams. These have nothing to do with the dreams of the world, though your dreams have brought about those dreams as well."

What is God's Will?

Candace: Holy Spirit, what is God's Will for us?

Holy Spirit: "God's Will is that you be restored in your thinking to the Truth of who and what you are. Because you are an extension of God, your will and God's Will are the same. Your Will is One. It cannot be different or separate. Your will then is to restore your mind to your Oneness with your Father and that includes your brothers and sisters. Your will and God's Will are the same. You never need doubt that.

"It is not God's Will that is directing you in the world. God's Will, in fact, is directing you out of the world. Generally speaking, it is the ego that is directing you in the world. In its fight for your autonomy, the ego is doing its job and fulfilling its function as you asked of it.

"There is the expression, 'Oops! I created a monster.' One may have had the intention to make a wonderful thing, some useful and meaningful thing, and without realizing the full ramifications of what they were making, they innocently made a monster. In a sense, that has been how the ego has served you. Ultimately, it certainly has fulfilled its purpose and function of giving you the gift of autonomy. Then there came a time when you said, 'Thank you. I am done with this gift.' And the ego said, 'I am not.' And that is where the pain and suffering began and compounded to the point of one needing to acknowledge it and do something about it.

"That is the beauty of making a monster. As in this case, there is the incredible motivation to overcome the ego and fight for your return to God. Before the monster was experienced, there was just the idea that one option would be to return Home. As the monster has become more prevalent, the desire for Oneness drives God's Children Home. It is establishing a force that is motivating God's Children with so much power that it will assist them in overcoming the world.

"God is waiting patiently where you left Him, with open arms and a loving heart, eagerly awaiting your return, and nothing you can do or will do could ever change that."

What is Truth?

Candace: Holy Spirit, what is Truth with a capital T?

Holy Spirit: "There appear to be several different levels of truth. God's Truth is the original Truth, as It was created and can't be changed, ever, under any circumstances. God's Truth is the one true Truth, and that would be the ultimate Truth that's true for everyone and that most people cannot see right now. This Truth allows there to be no right or wrong, good or bad, better or worse, only what is.

"God has never judged. God has no needs. God hasn't wanted anything. God hasn't expected anything. God just is and the Truths that go along with that are the simple Truths about your constant Perfection. You have never been anything other than Perfection, regardless of what you think you may have done in the world. You have never done anything wrong. You have never been separate. You are God's perfect Child.

"Then there are truths that are part of the illusion, what might be true for one or true for many. These are based primarily on perception rather than the true Truth of God. There are universal truths, 'Do unto others' and things like that, which are not God imposed types of truths. They are concepts that help you in having less to forgive yourself for, and again, forgiveness is not a God concept. There are many things that might be considered a universal truth. They might come from a higher place than other types of truths and yet, they're not true in God's mind.

"It's not a God truth that there is no time and space because in God's Reality there is no time or space. That is only man's reality. So man has to fabricate the truth that there is no time or space because man invented time and space. God doesn't have as a universal truth that there is no time and space because it simply doesn't exist. It doesn't need to even be addressed. You can have what's true for you. You can have your beliefs about God. You can have your beliefs about the world and about yourself, and those would be truths for you. Some of them may seem to be higher truths, and yet rarely would they be God Truths.

"When you begin to let down the wall that you have built between you and God and begin to join with God, so much of what you thought was truth falls away because it is only truth as perceived in the world, not Truth as perceived in God. If God is all there is and you have never strayed from God, it is hard to understand what could possibly be True in the world. Perhaps only your ability to have long and vivid dreams."

Chapter Highlights

"God is unconditionally loving because God is nothing else. God is only capable of seeing you as Perfection. You are not capable of being anything other than Perfection, except in your own mind."

———————

"God's Will is that you be restored in your thinking to the Truth of who and what you are. Because you are an extension of God, your will and God's Will are the same. Your Will is One."

———————

"When you begin to let down the wall that you have built between you and God and begin to join with God, so much of what you thought was truth falls away because it is only truth as perceived in the world, not Truth as perceived in God."

PART II

Hearing
God's Voice

"God's Children are the messengers
of His Message to each other."

5

What is Hearing God's Voice?

Holy Spirit: "God's Voice is the Gift that God gave to each of His Children as they stepped into the world. Hearing God's Voice is your most natural ability and It serves you unconditionally. God's Voice has one purpose and that is to restore you to the Truth of who you are, and It will do that in whatever ways you seek.

"Because there are only two voices to listen to, it becomes very easy to know when you are hearing God and when you are not. The challenge comes when you are not hearing this Voice and you want to choose differently, as well as hearing this Voice and applying what It says to your life. You can use this Voice to help you learn how to recognize It, how to choose It, and how to live It."

Candace's Story Continued

Candace: Six weeks after hearing the Holy Spirit in Muir Woods and deciding later that day to move to Hawaii, I landed on the Big Island. After settling into my new home overlooking Kealakekua Bay, I spent every morning swimming with the dolphins and would then go home and do my daily lesson from ACIM and meditate on the lanai for hours. I looked forward to the lessons and the ways that each one impacted my reality so deeply. My life was very sweet indeed.

While so much of the Course rang true to me, I did have one issue with it—the idea that one could not talk to God directly. The Course teaches that the Holy Spirit is the Voice for God, the go-between, the Translator, and that as long as we live in the world, we need the Holy Spirit to communicate with God. I didn't like this concept because I believed that I had been talking with God all my life. (Looking back on it now, I realize that all of my conversations with God were one-sided. I did all the talking. I felt God's Presence, and sensed that He was listening, but I never heard a response to any of my monologues.)

One day in late April, I was doing Course lesson 125, which was "In quiet I receive God's Word today." It starts like this: "Let this day be a day of stillness and of quiet listening. Your Father wills you hear His Word today. He calls to you from deep within your mind where He abides. Hear Him today. No peace is possible until His Word is heard around the world; until your mind, in quiet listening, accepts the message that the world must hear to usher in the quiet time of peace.... He has not waited until you return your mind to Him to give His Word to you. He has not hid Himself from you, while you have wandered off a little while from Him. He does not cherish the illusions which you hold about yourself.... Today He speaks to you. His Voice awaits your silence, for His Word can not be heard until your mind is quiet for a while and meaningless desires have been stilled. Await His Word in quiet."

So I did.

And in the quiet of meditation I heard, "Surrender to the Holy Spirit." I was not one to surrender, especially if I did not understand who I was surrendering to, so in my mind, I said, "No." A few minutes later that Voice said, "Surrender to the Holy Spirit." Again I resisted. This continued for a while until finally, and I do not know why, I surrendered. I surrendered to the Holy Spirit as well as to the idea that I could not talk with God directly.

It was literally as if a valve had opened and water came rushing in, flooding the space. The Voice flooded my mind, and I heard the most beautiful and loving communication about myself that I had ever heard before, and I knew that everything I heard was true even though I had never thought those things about myself. I asked this Voice who It was, and It told me that It was the Holy Spirit, which was the Voice for God. It was "the Voice" in lesson 125 that would share with me the Word of God.

During this experience, the only thing I was aware of in the world was this Voice. There was nothing else. The lanai was gone. The ocean was gone. It was such a tremendous feeling; I felt full and loved and at peace, while also thinking that I might explode. It seemed that I had felt this feeling before, though I don't know when or where, but I knew I wanted more of it. And I knew that it was true.

Then the Voice guided me to think of my best friend, and as I did, all of this amazing communication came into my mind about her. We had been best friends for a number of years by then, and yet these were things I had never noticed or thought about her, and they were all incredibly loving and true. Hearing these things about her allowed me to see her differently, and for the first time, I had the experience of really loving her unconditionally. A little while later, my housemate came home and I had the thought of him, and again, all of this communication came into my mind about him. It was incredibly loving and very true, and I had never noticed those things about him or seen him in that light.

Whenever my thoughts drifted off to other things, the Voice pulled me back to It. I continued to hear this Voice throughout the day and continued to be amazed by all of the communication I received and all of the things I became aware of. It was as if I had a friend sitting in my mind talking to me, making loving observations wherever we went. And it felt so comfortable and natural, as though I had just reconnected with a long lost friend, without the sense of any time having passed between us.

Later that day, I called DavidPaul and told him about my morning. I said, "You will never believe what happened to me!" He said, "Yes, I will" and listened patiently to the whole story. He was very excited and could feel that it was true. He called me back a few days later and told me that he was going to have a friend call, and he wanted me to give her communication from the Holy Spirit! He had been guided, without realizing it, to push me to share this Voice with others.

Needless to say, I was terrified at the thought of sharing this Voice, but for some reason, I agreed to share the Holy Spirit with her. We set up a time for her to call when we would both be free for an hour, which was three days later. While I was meditating before she called, I was guided to say a prayer of intention for our time together. The prayer that came to me as I waited was, "May it be with your blessings, God, that these words that come through are Yours and only Yours. May they bring joy and light to those who hear them and wisdom and knowledge to those who don't. Amen."

When this woman called, we spoke for a few minutes and then I told her that I would connect with the Holy Spirit and begin the session. I was very afraid and certain that I would have nothing to share with her, but since she was already on the phone, I had to proceed.

I said the prayer that I had been given and then I asked the Holy Spirit if It was willing to come through me. I heard, "Of course, precious one." I prayed to get out of the way, and then I began to see the Words of the Holy Spirit in front of my closed eyes. I read the Words out loud as they slowly appeared in front of me. It was a bit tortuous and yet exciting at the same time. Forty minutes quickly passed and the woman on the other end of the line was very happy, validated, and filled with a sense of peace about her life and her situation.

When we hung up, I jumped up and down and danced around the room. I was so excited that I was able to share the Holy Spirit with her and so grateful to be able to hear Truth. One thing I noticed was that the Words I shared with her were also applicable to me. Even though her situation was different than mine, the message of Truth and the perspective of Peace worked in my life as well. The Words that I shared changed the way I saw the world and the people in it....

What is Hearing God's Voice?

Candace: Holy Spirit, what does it mean to hear God's Voice?

Holy Spirit: "Hearing God's Voice can be hearing the wind blow by; it can be hearing music, hearing someone speak, hearing birds flying overhead; it can be a car horn or someone saying 'thank you' or 'I love you,' and it can be hearing specific Words that come from within your mind, within your own heart, that come from inside of you.

"The Holy Spirit is the Translator for God and acts as the Voice for God. The Holy Spirit communicates to you and through you using God's Voice, God's Mind, and your mind...providing comfort, guidance, direction, and love when you ask for it. It is something that isn't really offered unless it is asked for. The Holy Spirit is within you at all times and yet cannot give you guidance, comfort, or direction unless you have sought it.

"You may not have consciously said, 'Holy Spirit, please guide and direct me,' but you have, on some level, invited that guidance or direction in, and then you will hear it. It could be what you might sense as intuition, an inner voice, some kind of a conscience, some way that you know to turn left instead of right, or to not go to this particular place at this time. You are receiving guidance whether you consciously asked for it or not.

"You can hear God's Voice at any time under any circumstance. For many people, they find it easier to hear God's Voice when it's quiet, perhaps sitting down in somewhat of a meditative or reflective state without a lot of distractions.

And yet that might not be the time that you need to hear the Words the most. It may be that you are standing there with the world falling down around you and there is chaos, mayhem, and hysteria everywhere you look and you want to hear guidance and comfort and Truth. And, of course, there with the world crumbling down around you, you would want to go within and ask the Holy Spirit to join with you and communicate with you.

"As a daily practice it might be that you sit quietly, go within, and seek the Words without distraction so that you can be comfortable with what it is you are connecting with, how you are doing that, and the Voice that you hear, so that you know it is the Holy Spirit, and you know they are God's Words coming to you. You then have the opportunity to redevelop your faith and to reconnect with yourself and with God so that in a time of crisis you would have the confidence that what you are connecting with is, in fact, God's Voice.

"Say, for example, that the world is crumbling down around you. You might stand there and ask for Truth so that you can be reminded and reassured that there is no such thing as death. You might stand there asking for a perception of Truth that gives you peace as all of the chaos is carrying on around you, and you can know that you are, in fact, just watching an exciting movie and you need not be in fear. Or you might stand there with the world crumbling down around you and you might say, 'Holy Spirit, where do I run to be safe?' And you might be guided left or right or up or down to a safe physical place, as if there were such a thing.

"The Holy Spirit will join you where you are. The Holy Spirit will not say there is no such thing as 'safe' if that's what you are seeking, because the Holy Spirit will give you what you are seeking, which of course has nothing to do with deceiving you. If there is a 'safe' place for your body as the world is crumbling down around you, you will be guided to that place. And yet if you say, instead, 'I would rather have peace in this moment than fear,' the Holy Spirit will guide you to that as well. You may have the illusion that your fear is alleviated through the thought of a safe place to take cover, and yet that is temporary peace. Though if that's what you are seeking, that's what you will be given. That is one of the wonderful things about the Holy Spirit. The Holy Spirit will join with you where you are rather than expect you to be somewhere else.

"As you stand there seeking peace while the world is crumbling, in joining with God, in joining with the Holy Spirit, in seeking that which is Real, you will be delivered from your fear, delivered from your perceptions of fatality and destruction, and you will be brought into God's Arms, onto God's Lap and held and rocked and comforted. Your body may still be standing in all of the chaos and mayhem, and yet the body is what man made, not what God created. In Reality, it does not exist."

Hearing God Directly

Candace: Holy Spirit, is it possible to hear God directly?

Holy Spirit: "If one had no more barriers to Truth within them, they could hear God directly. That is a very big IF. When one no longer hears the ego and only hears the Holy Spirit, that is when the door becomes open to connect with God directly. At this point, with the ego so prevalent in the mind of God's Child, there needs to be a Translator, one who understands the ego and one who understands God, and the Holy Spirit fulfills this function perfectly.

"There are no barriers to Truth within the Holy Spirit, and the Holy Spirit can hear God directly. While those in the world have barriers to Truth, which are simply thoughts and beliefs, it is not possible to hear God directly. When one thinks they are hearing God, they are in fact hearing God's Voice and that is in effect the same as hearing God. It is just not hearing God directly. God is speaking to you and God is communicating with you through the Holy Spirit, so yes, you are hearing God and God is talking to you personally, and this is done through the Translator. Once those barriers are gone, the Translator will still exist, and yet It will no longer have that purpose. You will join with God directly."

The Evolution of Truth

DavidPaul: We believe that anyone can hear God's Voice, regardless of their state of mind or personal beliefs. For us, the longer we've been hearing this Voice, the more Truth we seem to receive. At the same time, the person who brought through *A Course in Miracles* seems to have brought through only Truth, with no previous experience of hearing Jesus's voice within her. Wanting to better understand why this is so, we asked the Holy Spirit.

Holy Spirit: "For the most part, when someone asks a question, they are looking for an answer that they can actually understand, an answer that makes sense to them, that they can take in and do something with. If someone asks you what 2 + 2 is and you answer with anything other than 4, you are most likely giving too much information, complicating the matter, and talking above where the person is. They have not asked, 'What is the meaning of 2 + 2?' They have not asked why 2 + 2 equals a particular number or anything else. They have just asked, 'What is 2 + 2?'

"When you ask a question of God or the Holy Spirit or Jesus, to present an answer other than what you have asked would not be of Truth. If you ask, 'What is the meaning of life?' or 'Why am I here?' there are at least six billion answers to those questions. The answer could be one thing on Monday and something different on Tuesday and something different next year because what you are asking for will be given to you and what you are truly asking at any given time can change.

"When you ask the Holy Spirit a question, you will get Truth every time. You will get as much Truth as you are truly asking for. You will get as much Truth as you can understand, take in, absorb, make sense of, work with, utilize, and apply, and no more. What would be the point of receiving more? It would be wasted and it would perhaps confuse any other Truth that might have otherwise been understood.

"If you were to say to the Holy Spirit, 'I want to receive communication that is above where I am right now. I want to receive the highest Truth,' you would not know if you were receiving the highest truth because you would not be able to understand the Truth in the message. When Jesus was delivering the Sermon on the Mount, so much Truth was shared on that day, and everyone heard something a little different depending on where they were. So the highest Truth might be told, and you will take from it what you can and nothing more. You cannot take more from it than you can understand. You may be given the highest Truth every time you connect with the Holy Spirit and what you can take from that is as much as you can understand in that moment.

"In looking at the person who brought through ACIM, which is an incredible piece of Truth, and yet perhaps in your understanding is beyond where the scribe's evolution was, in this case, she had a purpose. She had an agreement with Jesus and an understanding that she would perform a service and do a job. Her agreement was to take dictation for Jesus, and yet little by little, she absorbed.

"Each person has their own mission and purpose in the world that is just for them. And whatever they do for them, in Truth, benefits the Sonship. It has no other choice. So, if this person who brought through ACIM fulfills her function, she does that for you, not because you now have a book to read but because when another fulfills their true function, they do it for all.

"You can give thanks to that person and to the countless others who today are able to look upon another and see them without judgment, to see them with love and acceptance, to see them as a Child of God, as their Brother. You can give thanks for that person who puts the effort and the intention and the desire into looking upon another with eyes of Truth. At the end of every day, you can give thanks for all of the people who saw the world, not through the body's eyes, but through God's Eyes. You can give thanks for all of the people who chose not to judge but to love instead. You can give thanks for every person who saw Love where there was hatred, or Peace where there was pain, for every person who chose Joy over suffering, for everyone who chose to see the Truth today over the illusion of the world, and for each one who was not tricked by the ego or deceived by that part of their mind but chose Reality instead. You can give thanks for everyone who chose differently today, who did so on your behalf. No greater gift could they give you."

Exercise—Focusing on Kindness

Holy Spirit: "When one looks around in the world, more often than not, one notices pain and suffering, crime and punishment, anger and resentment, selfishness and inconsideration…. These are the things that make the news and as such, they are what one puts their attention on or becomes aware of. The habit in the world is to notice these things when, in fact, most of what is occurring in the world is kindness and cooperation, love and appreciation, courtesy and gratitude, care and respect.

"As you go out into the world today, make note of all of the ways that you notice people being cooperative—people who take turns at stop signs, people who wait patiently in lines, people who serve those waiting in lines. Notice how many people do kind and courteous, thoughtful and caring deeds throughout the course of the day…whether it be holding open a door; greeting someone with a smile, a look, or perhaps a hello; when one allows someone to go ahead of them on the street or in a line; when someone helps another, is kind to another, or gives something to another.

"It is easy to see the person sitting on the sidewalk asking for money or help and to focus on the problems of the world, homelessness and suffering and this type of thing, and to not notice the people who come up to give this person money or food or a kind word. The opportunity for those people to give is a tremendous gift, and the one who is asking is offering that gift.

"As you go about your life in the world today, notice all of the kindness, courtesy, and cooperation and focus on how much of that is occurring. Rather than the 1 in 50 times that someone is rude to another, focus on the 49 out of 50 encounters where people are kind or respectful or courteous. Focus on that which is of Right-Mindedness, Love, and Truth, and remember that even when you see that 1 out of 50, or 1 out of 100, or 1 out of 500 encounters that might be rude, remember that it is just a cry for help."

The Difference between Channeling and Hearing God's Voice

DavidPaul: Over the years, we have read a number of spiritual books based on Truth. Many of these books were channeled communications from ones such as Mother Mary, Jesus, Emmanuel, Ramtha, Bartholomew, and others, and they all inspired us in unique ways. Some might perceive hearing the Holy Spirit as a form of channeling, but after many years of hearing this Voice, this is not our experience. To help explain the difference between channeling (hearing other voices of Truth) and hearing the Holy Spirit, we asked the Holy Spirit for clarification.

Holy Spirit: "All of the definitions overlap here and there, but what is important is that you hear Truth, that you seek Truth, that you follow Truth, and move in the direction of Truth. Since it is difficult to hear God directly, the Holy Spirit is a Voice that has been instilled within each person to be a Translator between that person and God. God is this giant mass and within God are you and everyone else. You are a part of God. The Holy Spirit is a part of you. The Holy Spirit is within you and you are within God.

"God put the Translator right inside of you where you could not lose It and gave you full and complete access to It. The Holy Spirit is this direct line, and It is there for you to hear in a way that you won't hear other things. You cannot 'channel' the Holy Spirit because It is a part of you and within you. There is nothing to channel. You are just tuning in to a particular frequency of your Self and communicating that frequency just as you would change stations on a radio.

You might hear your thinking on this; you might hear your thinking on that; you might hear your mother's voice at times; you might hear your self at a different time or your self now; and you might hear the Holy Spirit. At different times you will hear different things within yourself, and it is just tuning into different frequencies.

"In asking about other spirits who are speakers of Truth, there are many who can either hear the Holy Spirit themselves or who have a grasp on Truth and will share it. If this works for you, so be it. What you are looking for ultimately is your own direct communication. For those who hear God in their own way, that is wonderful. For those who do not, the Holy Spirit is there for them as God's Translator. Then if you add more translators to that, in particular, ones that are not literally installed within you, you are getting a less quality translation. The Holy Spirit is a direct translator that is a part of you, rather than something that is not a part of you. Not to say that things are separate in Truth, but to say that your own unique, direct connection to God is already there within you. Using a different one will not quite be the same. Use what works for you, and perhaps all of the things one might use along the way are steps toward that end. It is the seeking that matters, not necessarily the end result.

"If you were to get a sign, to literally see a sign that gives you the direction that you've been asking about, if you hear something, if you read something, if someone tells you something that you have a sense is meant for you or is a Message for you, it doesn't matter where it comes from. You have a knowing within you that, in fact, this is a Message and to take heed. Whether it be from God, the Holy Spirit, or your Right-Mind, it is a way of serving you, guiding and directing you—perhaps hitting you over the head, perhaps doing what it takes because you've been seeking and haven't noticed the answers. You continue to seek and continue to seek and the answers continue to elude you, when in fact, they've been there all along. These 'forces for good' will conspire to move you along in the direction that you seek. It is irrelevant or inconsequential who or how or what, just that this combined force for good would give you that which you are seeking. The universe simply operates that way. It has no choice.

"Continue to seek Truth. Continue to seek Right-Mindedness, God-Mind, that which can truly serve you in your heart and mind and know that you will ultimately have that which you seek, and how you get there is irrelevant."

People of Different Faiths

DavidPaul: Holy Spirit, how do people of different faiths work with You?

Holy Spirit: "Regardless of what faith or whom one believes in, whenever one hears Truth, they are communicating with the Holy Spirit. If someone is practicing any religion, whoever the Source or Creator within that religion may be, if one is communicating with that Source or with the Translator for that Source, it is the same; it is the Holy Spirit.

"Every single thing in the world is an illusion. Every single religion—Judaism, Christianity, Islam, Hinduism, Buddhism, and so on—is an illusion. None of it exists, so it is not necessary to speak about other religions specifically in the sense of acknowledging or distinguishing one from another. Regardless of who you think you are praying to, with, for, or about, there is only one true Creator, which, in this form, we are calling God. And you may call God whatever you prefer.

"For those who have been able to hear the Holy Spirit and ask It its name, they have brought the recognition of the Holy Spirit, by that name, into the world. Once it hits the world, any name is as good as another, and yet the Creator has called this Voice the Holy Spirit and has offered It to everyone equally.

"Within the world, all of God's children have the opportunity to pursue whatever path, belief, religion, god, and/or faith that they desire, and yet behind every one is the same Source. Behind every one is the same Truth. Behind every one is the Reality that all of this is but a dream, and the illusion that is the world does not exist. Know that regardless of what you call 'Source,' anything you hear that is True, anything you hear that is Right-Minded, loving, or kind, comes from God through God's Voice or Interpreter by whatever name It is called. It matters not *what* It is called, just so long as It is called."

Chapter Highlights

"The Holy Spirit is the Translator for God and acts as the Voice for God. The Holy Spirit communicates to you and through you using God's Voice, God's Mind, and your mind...providing comfort, guidance, direction, and love when you ask for it."

———

"If one had no more barriers to Truth within them, they could hear God directly....At this point, with the ego so prevalent in the mind of God's Child, there needs to be a Translator, one who understands the ego and one who understands God, and the Holy Spirit fulfills this function perfectly."

———

"When you ask the Holy Spirit a question, you will get Truth every time. You will get as much Truth as you are truly asking for. You will get as much Truth as you can understand, take in, absorb, make sense of, work with, utilize, and apply, and no more."

———

"You cannot 'channel' the Holy Spirit because it is a part of you and within you. There is nothing to channel. You are just tuning in to a particular frequency of your self and communicating that frequency just as you would change stations on a radio."

———

"Regardless of what faith or whom one believes in, whenever they hear Truth, they are communicating with the Holy Spirit."

6

The Gifts of Hearing

"When we look through eyes of Love,
we see a world of Love beaming back at us."

Holy Spirit: "When one begins to really hear God's Voice and begins to listen in such a way as to benefit from what they are hearing, the gifts of this experience are indescribable. Hearing and not hearing is the difference between sleeping and being truly awake, quite literally. When one is not hearing this Voice, they are sleepwalking through their life. As one begins to hear and to listen, they begin to come alive, and the Truth of who and what they are begins to direct their life in such a way as to truly live.

"It is easy to follow the path of least resistance when you are sleepwalking, yet when you are awake, alive, and moving, really being pulled Home, your life takes on meaning, purpose, and satisfaction in ways you have only dreamed of, in ways you have never even dreamed of. As you live a life based on Truth, you recognize who you are, you recognize who the one in front of you is, and you understand why you are here, where you are going, what is Real, and what has just been a dream. Only Peace and Love and Joy exist within that, and despite how you may have been living up to now, that is truly all you seek."

Candace's Story Continued

Candace: DavidPaul continued to send people to me to share the Holy Spirit with, and others soon found me as well. As time went on, I made a commitment

53

to never offer or suggest that someone receive communication from the Holy Spirit. If someone was meant to have a session, somehow it would come up. There were times when I was in line at the grocery store or hanging out at the beach, and strangers would start talking to me about wanting to connect with God, or feeling disconnected from Source, or needing more guidance and direction in their lives. At those times, I would tell people about my work with the Holy Spirit and each one would ask for a session. I knew these people were sent to me from the Holy Spirit and I was grateful to be sharing the Voice with them.

I also made a commitment to always say yes to any request to hear from the Holy Spirit. I encountered many people who wanted to hear this Voice within themselves, and I worked with others who just wanted to be given the answers to their problems. This was frustrating for me because I really wanted to help others hear the Voice of God within them rather than solve their problems. I wanted to "teach a man to fish" rather than catch a fish for him every day.

Over time, hearing this Voice became a regular part of my life. Oftentimes I would be sitting with friends on the beach or taking a break on a hike and we would decide to tune in to the Voice. On many of those occasions, Jesus or Mary would come through me instead of the Holy Spirit. They would introduce themselves and communicate specific things related to those personalities. In a way, I preferred this because I was still uncomfortable with Who and What the Holy Spirit was. I found that many people were unfamiliar with the Holy Spirit, yet they had a deep affinity for Mary or Jesus. Eventually, as I became more comfortable with the Holy Spirit, Jesus and Mary stopped coming through me.

I came to realize that my job was to share the Holy Spirit by name and to help others become comfortable with God's Voice in that form. One way to do that was to write a book about hearing the Holy Spirit. Writing a book wasn't my idea, but I was tuning in to the Voice every morning and writing down what I heard, and one morning I was given a book title. It was, *Planting a Garden within Your Heart and Mind to Sow God's Seeds of Love*—this would be a manual for hearing God's Voice in all that you do. Not knowing the first thing about how to write a book, I continued to write down the guidance I received and waited for more direction.

A little over a year after I first heard the Holy Spirit, DavidPaul was feeling very frustrated because he really wanted to hear this Voice for himself, so I was guided to hold "playshops," which were workshops that were not supposed to be serious. In these workshops I would share the Voice of the Holy Spirit with a group, which included anywhere from 8 to 40 people, and then answer any questions. Afterward, we did different activities designed to spark that Voice or help one recognize what they might already be hearing.

I found that many people had experience with a 'voice,' but they had trouble discerning whose voice it was or trusting the integrity of the message. We practiced using God's Voice and testing and trusting our intuition so we could strengthen our ability to be guided. Many people had sought a tangible connection with God, and by doing the exercises in the playshops, had been able to ascribe certain experiences, signs, and messages as coming from God. It was very exciting....

Peace and Comfort

Candace: Holy Spirit, what are the benefits to hearing your Voice?

Holy Spirit: "Even though God's children live in the world and have forgotten their Oneness with God, there is still an inkling, a seedling, something left within each child that causes them to have a tiny bit of the memory that, in fact, they are One with God. Even with all of the thoughts and beliefs that they have acquired that have caused them to think that they are unworthy, God is unworthy, God isn't real, they are fine on their own, or whatever beliefs that keep them from remembering fully, despite all of that, there's still this inkling within them that they are One with God. Somewhere deep down, they remember that God is their true Creator, their true Source, and Who they yearn to return Home to.

"For some, it seems that the journey would be impossibly long, even though it is just a thought away. For others, it seems that their Oneness with God was only a transition—that was then and this is now and they have moved on from God. There are 6 billion thoughts and then some that would keep one from God, and yet this tiny spark of remembrance of that Oneness keeps them thinking about God, keeps them trying to understand God, trying to come up with a belief system around God that works for them, trying to make God real, and so on. There is a pull within each of God's Children toward this end, and in the opportunity to hear God, one can remember Truth.

"The words, the perspective, and the love that comes through the Holy Spirit from God are a reassurance and a promise for that restoration to one day be complete. You are the only one keeping you from it. You are already perfect, worthy, and fully and completely loved by God; you just have to eventually remember that. Whether it is in this instant, or this instant, or this instant, it doesn't matter. In each instant that you can remember, you are born. The idea of one being born again and again and again in each moment that you remember your Oneness with God is the true definition of being 'born again.' You are born in Reality, not the world.

"Truly, one gains everything by hearing God because there is no Reality in the world. When one hears God, they are in Reality for that moment. When one hears God, they experience validation or proof of what they have always known somewhere in the back of their mind, no matter how buried that knowing may be beneath the accumulated thoughts and beliefs that say otherwise. Hearing God proves to the little spark of hope that was there all along, that there is more to life than this.

"It is so easy to live in the world, to attempt to succeed and excel in school, to succeed and excel in work, to make the perfect family, home, and lifestyle. 'Lifestyle' here means the right place to live, the right home, the right furnishings, right car, clothing, vacations, or the right entertainment system. One goes about continuing to accomplish, attain, succeed, and excel in all of these worldly ways until they die. And so many people walk around in the world saying, 'Isn't there more to life than this?'

"This is just a game that one plays for fun, for learning, for different experiences. This is not reality. When one can hear God, they can step out of the need to strive, excel, and succeed, and in fact seek peace and love in their hearts, in their minds, in their lives, in their relationships, and in the world so that the life they are living is one that is an expression of God, that is an awareness and a remembering of the Oneness that you are with God. This allows you to live a life that has meaning in so many of the moments, encounters, and experiences rather than in the things.

"It is not that one must sit and worship God in a church, a God that looks like this and thinks like that. When one talks about false idols, they are talking about the belief that striving toward the perfect entertainment system is more important than striving toward expressing kindness toward their family. People put much more energy and resources into the perfect entertainment system than they do into showing their family that they love them. Some think they are showing their family that they love them by buying them the right entertainment system. When one has learned that joy or happiness comes from a screen and they experience love when they watch a story on that screen, then it makes sense that the perfect entertainment system is a wonderful way to love one's family.

"Ultimately, what each one seeks from the bottom of their hearts is God's Love, true Love, the remembrance of their Oneness, the remembrance that God is everything, God is good, and they are within God always, safe and sound, loved and cherished, accepted and understood just as they are. To sit with God with that perspective is so much more fulfilling and rewarding than anything that is on the screen.

"What does one gain from hearing God? They gain themselves. They gain God. They gain everything that really is, everything that really matters, and with that, all the peace and comfort that they can experience."

Guidance and Direction

Holy Spirit: "With the opportunity to experience God, to hear God's Words, and to receive Truth as guidance and direction, it is literally like being handed a map when you are out in a million acre forest and have no idea where you are or how to get out. You suddenly stumble upon a map, then you hit the trail and you are able to very efficiently, directly, and smoothly find your way home. It is the same with this Voice; all one needs is the guidance and the direction to restore their mind to Truth, which then puts them right in their Oneness with God. It is just like being handed a map, and that is what the Holy Spirit is in Truth, a map."

Candace: Over the years, DavidPaul and I have sought guidance and insight from the Holy Spirit on life altering decisions as well as the most mundane topics imaginable. As a couple, these questions have ranged from how to write a wedding ceremony and prepare for having a child to when to sell stock, how to "sleep train" our daughter, or which vitamin and mineral supplements to take, if any. God does not have an agenda for what we seek guidance and help with. The Holy Spirit will join us wherever we are—from how to deal with PMS to understanding the Universe.

Hearing the Holy Spirit has been so incredibly rewarding for both of us that it's hard to imagine living our lives without It. The following story of how David-Paul and I became a couple is an example of the blessing that hearing this Voice has been in our lives.

Candace's Story Continued

Candace: After living in Hawaii for several years, I woke up one morning with the realization that I wanted to be married and have children. This was a surprise to me, as well as to my boyfriend. Though we loved each other and planned to be married 'in the future,' as it turned out, the future was something that was never going to come.

While I was wondering what to do about this dilemma, a friend needed a house sitter for a few weeks, so I moved out to clear my mind and seek guidance and direction. Though I was listening to the Voice of the Holy Spirit within me, it was hard to trust that what I heard was true because I didn't like what I heard—that my boyfriend was not my life partner.

I called DavidPaul to tell him where he could reach me for the next few weeks. The next day he called to tell me that he had been in love with me for some time and wanted to make a life with me. I had sensed this at some point, but the reality of it was quite a surprise. He was 6 years younger than me, and I had always considered him my little brother. We were very close, on very similar paths, and we shared a lot of love between us, but marriage and family seemed impossible.

Confused and unsure, I asked the Holy Spirit for guidance and direction, but because I thought I knew what was best for me, I continued to doubt what I heard. I was then guided by the Holy Spirit to watch for signs and let them direct my path instead.

Immediately, one of my jobs ended and another slowed to a crawl. My living situation changed and my boyfriend decided definitively that he could not commit to marriage and children. I then had a run of massage clients from Silicon Valley, where DavidPaul had moved to, who all told me what a wonderful place it was. Shortly thereafter, DavidPaul sent me a one way plane ticket to visit him, with the understanding that I could return to the island any time I wanted. And when I inquired about putting my things in storage, there were no storage units available on the island.

As this momentum built, I received the following communication from the Holy Spirit:

Holy Spirit: "Greetings and blessing to you precious one. Indeed this is a special day. We haven't communicated in this way (writing in my journal) in some time. How are you? We've missed you.

"Your life is a funny one right now. I hope you are not taking it seriously. Of course you are supposed to see DavidPaul. He was sent to you a long time ago. Remember? He is a gift to you for all of your hard work—and vice verse. It is possible that you could make something work with each other. How badly do you want it? God's Will is one thing, but it is your desire that brings about all that you have in your life. First is the desire, then the goal, then the attainment of the goal.

"Due to free will, God cannot intend for your path to be something other than what you want. It is only that many have forgotten what it is they asked for before they came here to Earth, and God is a reminder about that intention. God keeps you on the path you planned for yourself before you arrived in the body. God's Will is that you be happy. Not at the expense of others, but for the benefit of others. If you have something that would make you so happy and also be of benefit to others, of course that would be God's Will for you. It is not His Will that you suffer, remember? It is only your belief in suffering and the need for it that would bring that about in your life. You have already learned all there is to know about suffering. This is a lifetime of joy, play, celebration, rejoicing...and that is what the two of you will do together. Of course, there will be difficult times, times where there is discord, confusions, hurts, resentments, but no more than there is now for DavidPaul while he is alone and not benefiting from the opportunity to join with another. And no more than there is for you in the relationship you are completing, yet without the same opportunities for joy.

"It is essential that you both be vulnerable, open, honest, sweet, loving, innocent, and as little children in this process because then God can work through you to show you how to be with each other. You have never been with anyone like the other and it will be different indeed. God bless you both in this journey and know of course that We are with you always, loving you, guiding you, laughing with you, and showing you the way.

"Blessings. Amen."

Candace: The signs and communication continued like this until finally I knew that I was supposed to leave paradise and move to California to explore the possibility of a life with DavidPaul. Despite the fact that I planned on never leaving Hawaii, with the guidance and the signs that I received from the Holy Spirit, I didn't doubt my decision and I never looked back....

Understanding

DavidPaul: Hearing the Holy Spirit has also helped us to deepen our understanding about life, ourselves, and our personal truths in a profound way. A small but eye-opening example of this unfolded while I was writing the following paragraph.

I wrote: "We have had a yearning in our hearts for a long time to share the Words of the Holy Spirit with others. Even though God sees only our Perfection and does not validate the illusion of separation that we have made in our minds,

He is joyful when we open up to receiving the love that He has for us, when we hear His Voice, and create a fulfilling relationship with Him. He wants to communicate with us. We have known in our hearts for a long time that sharing the Voice of the Holy Spirit and supporting others in hearing this Voice within them was our service this lifetime."

After completing this paragraph, something just didn't feel right, so I asked the Holy Spirit for some feedback. This is what I heard:

Holy Spirit: "All projection. It's not possible for God to be joyful or not based on what you do. God *is* joyful, period. It may help you to be joyful when you connect with God in that way or when you connect with you, but it is not possible to do something that would make God happy. That's one of the paradoxes in relationship with God. So many people live their lives wanting and trying and yearning and striving toward doing that which would make God happy. There are entire religions devoted to it, masses of people aspiring to that end, and yet there is nothing that anyone could do or not do that could make God happy or not. God just is, and God is not the effect of you. You can put in your statement, 'God is happy, and it seems that we are happy when we do these things,' and that would be the point. God already is happy and doesn't need to do anything to become happier."

DavidPaul: So God doesn't have any desire for us to hear His Voice?

Holy Spirit: "Ultimately, no."

DavidPaul: So why did He give us the Holy Spirit?

Holy Spirit: "For you, not for Him. For His Children who have gone on their way so that they can find their way back Home. That has nothing to do with God being happy or not happy."

DavidPaul: So God doesn't even *want* us to find our way home?

Holy Spirit: "God doesn't have an agenda for you to find your way Home. God is not going to be happy or unhappy because of what you do. That doesn't necessarily mean that God wouldn't want you to be rejoined with God in your thinking. God loves you in the way that can allow you to be where you are because God loves what *is*. Why would God want for something? God has no agenda for His Children because God understands that they have never been separate. God understands that they have never strayed, only in their minds. So what could God want for them when they're already perfect and they're already at One with Him? There is nothing more to want for His Children.

"Even to say that God wants your happiness is a projection. *You* want your happiness. You think that may come from a connection with God, so it is projected onto God, 'God wants my happiness and that can be achieved through a connection between the two of us. And God will be happy if there is a connection between the two of us.' However, in Reality, God just loves you. Wherever you are, whatever you're doing, whatever you're thinking, whatever you believe, God just loves you. God hasn't gone anywhere and neither have you. There are just a few beliefs and thoughts between you and God. That's all.

"God is everything and you are a part of God, and because you judge certain things about yourself, certain parts of you, you have the idea that God can judge you as well, as a part of Him. But this doesn't happen. There are no expectations, no hopes, no dreams, no goals, no agendas for God's Children. All God's Children have free will to go out into the world or not and seek their fortunes or not, pursue their dreams or not, and God does not have the idea, one way or the other, that this is right or wrong.

"God just watches what you do and looks through eyes of love and is able to understand why you do what you do, so there is no need for you to do something else. If you are happy, that's fine. If you are not happy, that's fine. That has nothing to do with God. It is your choice in every moment to perceive God or not, experience God or not, acknowledge God or not. It is your choice in any and every moment to be happy or not, to live in the world or to live in Truth. Reality is just one thought away."

Exercise—The Truth of God

Holy Spirit: "Take a few minutes to contemplate God. After doing so, make a list of all the things that you think God is and then keep writing until you cannot think of anything else that God is. For example:

1.   God is all powerful.

2.   God is loving.

3.   God is vengeful.

4.   God is real (or God is unreal).

5.   And so on....

"The list could be a hundred items long if that is what occurs to you about what God is. Then go over your list and notice in what ways are *you* the things that you wrote down.

"God is all powerful—In what ways are *you* all powerful? The truth is, in the world, you make the world. And in that sense, *you* are all powerful in that you make your reality. God does not create it for you.

"God is vengeful—In what ways or at what times are *you* vengeful? Maybe it is just a thought that you want someone to get what they deserve, or this type of thing. But even if it is 'just a thought,' that is equally as powerful as an action.

"In what ways are you loving? In what ways are you real or unreal? Begin to notice that everything you believe God is, is really what you believe you are, at least sometimes, or in certain situations, or in your thinking. And when you have finished going over your list, imagine for a moment that God does not have the ego and God does not think with the Holy Spirit. God is just Truth, and from the highest worldly perception imaginable, God is Love. And begin to notice for yourself the Truth of Who God might be, rather than who you think God is."

True Religion

Candace: The Holy Spirit continually reminds DavidPaul and I to live the Truth that we are given. Hearing or knowing the Truth is not the hard part; it's applying the Truth to our lives and how we live that is often difficult for us.

Holy Spirit: "What people truly seek is a way to live their lives so that moment to moment, hour to hour, day to day, and year to year, they are happy, fulfilled, contented, and at peace with themselves, their mind, their life, and the world. Applying the Holy Spirit to your life is what will give you that. No pill, no program, no book, no religion, other than your own true religion, will give you that.

"In making the commitment to hear God's Voice within you and in making the decision to hear God's Voice outside of you, you then live in Heaven. Wherever God is, there is Heaven. And if God's Voice is all you hear, then you must be in Heaven.

"When you hear God's Voice and use that Voice in how you live, you are able to know Truth and easily make decisions and move in whatever direction you are guided. When you make a decision about how you want to live, when you commit to Peace over pain and Truth over illusion, it is very simple to know how to live in each moment and in every situation. Your own true religion is knowing yourself, knowing God and God's Will for you, believing and trusting in that, and allowing the Holy Spirit to translate the language of the world into God's language, so that you may be that which you *are*, which is Love.

"Hearing God's Voice is always available to everyone, unconditionally. Choosing to hear this Voice is the key. Choosing is up to you. In Truth, you don't have a choice about God's Will. You don't have a choice about God's Voice or about that Voice being within you or a part of you. But you can choose not to hear, and that is the key. Beyond the choosing is the living. And it is dedication to choosing and living a certain way that allows you to experience the Truth of who you are."

————

Candace: It was on Christmas day, 1997, when we first received communication from the Holy Spirit about discovering and living our true religion:

Holy Spirit: "Greetings and blessings to you precious ones. Indeed this is a holy day and a most joyous occasion that we would gather together in this way on this most sacred of days. Every day can be this for you. Every day can be a holy day. Every day can be a sacred day. Today is one in which there is agreement on this. It is true that it is amazing that the world over is celebrating the anniversary of Jesus's birth today when perhaps on other days, most around the world would say that they don't even believe He ever existed or exists now or is in fact living in their hearts and minds. And yet there is some powerful momentum occurring within each one that builds and builds until this day comes when there is the understanding that 'Peace on Earth, Goodwill toward Men' is indeed the ultimate. That each person would treat each other a little differently, that each one would be a little kinder, that each one would be a little more generous, if only for one day or one time of year, is a miracle indeed.

"The stories of scrooges being transformed into very generous people are stories that tend to occur only during this season. It is a season of transforming many of the aspects of yourself which you are not deeply in love with into aspects of yourself which you deeply love. It is a time of transforming all the areas of your life into exactly what you want them to be, so that what one is doing during this holy season is practicing a way to live—practicing kindness.

"This is expressed by allowing someone to go ahead of them on the street, or in their cars, or through a doorway. Donating money to good causes, donating time to be of service, being more honorable or charitable or more in integrity in their work or generous in their deeds, the opportunity to not hold onto certain seeming injustices and to simply let them go, to move on…are all examples of this. To show appreciation to those they love by purchasing things for them are acts of love to demonstrate their feelings…to communicate with them, spend time with them, share words with family and friends that perhaps are not said throughout the year; and between lovers, to communicate those words that are often taken for granted or are presumed said when in fact the words are so lovely to hear.

"This is a time of year to practice how one would want to be in all areas of their life. To plant the seeds of the perfection of the world during this time of year can carry you through into the next year with the practice of kindness being at the foundation of your life.

"When one attends a church service, it feels like a *moment* of honoring something that is perhaps important, and yet *living* a lifestyle and practice of what is important to you is your religion. Many would say, 'I am not religious. I am spiritual.' In a way this is not taking ownership or responsibility for a way of living. When one says their religion is Catholicism or Judaism, they are saying, 'This is how I live.' They are not saying, 'This is a church service I have sat through, or a book I have read, or something my family spoke of,' but a way of living.

"When one is Catholic, they have certain prayers and masses and ritual and ceremony that they undertake on a day-to-day basis, such as praying the rosary, taking Holy Communion, joining only in marriage, and so on. Doing certain things on certain days of the week is a way of honoring that which one sees as sacred, a way of honoring that which one believes God has created. Whether or not you agree with what they do, it is a way of life; it is making a lifestyle around what one believes to be important.

"Even if you do not agree with another's priorities, when one holds these priorities as high for themselves, to live this lifestyle is to live in honor and integrity and in grace with God through intention. There are many varieties of Christianity. Some include certain tenets around marriage and family and other things, and this would be based on priorities—personal, individual priorities and values. Holy practices and beliefs are what bring about a sense of honor and tradition and connectedness for so many.

"To say that one is spiritual is to say that you are inherently an aspect of God. What does that look like as a lifestyle? What does that look like as a path? What practices does that involve so that you are living the lifestyle of 'spirituality?' Do you see that when you say 'I am spiritual and not religious' that this is a way to avoid commitment to a certain lifestyle? One would say 'I am not religious because I am not Bible-oriented' and these kinds of things, and yet that is not the true definition of religion.[1] These are ways to escape the commitment to a lifestyle that you truly desire to make.

"Perhaps today your goal would be to gently and lovingly notice what your priorities are. What is important to you? What matters to you? What feels like something you would not want to live without? Make a mental note of this and at the end of the day or as it occurs to you, you can make note of these priorities. Perhaps as you allow these to unfold you can discuss them and think about what would be your true religion. What would be a lifestyle and a way of practicing that which you love and that which is important to you and that which brings meaning to your life? How can you have ritual and ceremony and these sorts of things in such a way that you feel you have your true religion? It does not matter the name you call it. It does not matter what form it takes, only to think how you might like to live.

"For the Dalai Lama, his true religion is kindness. You can see how every moment he would be able to ascertain, 'What would be the best way to honor my religion in this moment?' And of course, that would be the kindest behavior in that moment. Now, sometimes, his religion can be difficult, because what may be the most kind in that moment may not look the most kind. Is it the most kind to you or is it the most kind to the other person? Is it the most kind to the planet, the most kind to God? Who is this kindness extended to?

"The dilemma comes in when, in Truth, the kindness must be originated toward self in order that it be extended outward as a result of the kindness extended inward. If your true religion is kindness, you must do what is most kind for yourself in each moment. Now it may be that what is being most kind for yourself is to deny yourself something or to experience something you might rather not for the sake of another. You can see how there is a continuous double-edged sword in the religion of kindness. Sometimes you must be kind to yourself and deny the other and sometimes kindness is denying yourself to give to the other. This is a constant challenge for one whose religion in kindness.

"It would seem that it would be simple to discern what would be kind in every moment, and yet, it goes so much deeper—kind for whom, kind in what way,

---

1.   Merriam-Webster Dictionary (1) the service and worship of God or the supernatural
   (2) commitment or devotion to religious faith or observance
   (3) a personal set or institutionalized system of religious attitudes, beliefs, and practices
   (4) a cause, principle, or system of beliefs held to with ardor and faith

kind in that moment or kind over a lifetime, kind toward one's evolution or kind toward that present moment?

"Let's say there are two people who have been in an accident. They have both stopped breathing. Which one do I give CPR to first? To whom would it be kind to give CPR? And which one would be the kindest? If these people have tuberculosis or some life threatening communicable disease, would it be kind for me to give them CPR and put my life in danger?

"Having to determine in each moment what is kindness may not be as easy as one might think. What does kindness really mean? You may think it is kind to solve a problem for another person when in fact it could be the cruelest thing you do that day or week or lifetime because that person's mission or purpose for this whole lifetime was to figure out how to solve that problem on their own.

"The Dalai Lama's true religion can be a source throughout his lifetime of discerning at every opportunity what is for the highest good of all. That is the way in which he serves himself in every situation. Develop your own religion and over time you will have this opportunity as well to determine, based on your priorities and your religion, what is truly for the highest good of all. You will be given this opportunity in every moment; it will be up to you to choose it.

"Think about your priorities and make note of what they are. It is most important that you follow what is true for you, not what you think might be true for another, or what might please another, and certainly not what you think will please God. If you choose something, a priority, a goal, a lifestyle, or a religion to please God, in the end it will never work. You will have failed. And all your efforts will be for naught. Allow your priorities to unfold, and know that there is not a predetermined set or list that you must have. There are only those which are true in your heart."

Chapter Highlights

"What does one gain from hearing God? They gain themselves. They gain God. They gain everything that really is, everything that really matters, and with that, all the peace and comfort they can experience."

———

"With the opportunity to experience God, to hear God's Words, and to receive Truth as guidance and direction, it is literally like being handed a map when you are out in a million acre forest and have no idea where you are or how to get out."

———

"Wherever you are, whatever you're doing, whatever you're thinking, whatever you believe, God just loves you. God hasn't gone anywhere and neither have you. There are just a few beliefs and thoughts between you and God. That's all."

———

"What people truly seek is a way to live their lives so that moment to moment, hour to hour, day to day, and year to year, they are happy, fulfilled, contented, and at peace with themselves, their mind, their life, and the world. Applying the Holy Spirit to your life is what will give you that. No pill, no program, no book, no religion, other than your own true religion, will give you that."

7

The Barriers to Hearing God's Voice

"Though it is only a thought
and not a step
that will bring you Home,
God is with you on the journey."

Holy Spirit: "Because hearing God's Voice is your most natural state, it is easy to wonder what keeps you from It. In Truth, it is only a thought, a thought of separation, a thought of unworthiness, a thought that It is not real; and with that thought, God's Voice is gone from you.

"Fortunately, it is only a thought. Fortunately, it only takes a thought to bring the Voice back to you—the thought that the Holy Spirit is part of you, that God's Voice is your right, that God gave this to you unconditionally. With those thoughts, you open the door to Truth.

"Your mind just thinks. You can choose the thoughts you want to make real, and you can ignore the rest. The Holy Spirit can help you discern which thoughts you want to keep and which ones you want to ignore until eventually you will only think thoughts of Truth. You will only think with the Holy Spirit."

Candace's Story Continued

Candace: When I first heard the Holy Spirit within me back in Hawaii, It was a constant companion that I could join with and listen to. I felt a sense of belonging when I heard God's Voice, and that feeling of being alone in the world was gone. It was a wonderful comfort and a constant reassurance of the Truth of who I am.

As time went on, I continued doing sessions with others since I had committed in the beginning to always say yes. Each time I shared a Message from the Holy Spirit with someone, I would find that the Message was true for me as well. Most of the sessions I did with people also included guidance on how to hear God's Voice in the world. Because the Messages were equally applicable to me and because I could already hear this Voice, I thought that hearing this Voice was all I needed. I came to believe that sharing this Voice with others was enough to keep my own life on track and I soon stopped hearing this Voice within me on my own.

I would tune into the Holy Spirit for a session with someone else and then "turn It off" when I was done. Before long, I was no longer listening to the Holy Spirit throughout the day and I began to become more enmeshed in the world and lose my foothold in Reality. I forgot who I was and why I was here, and I forgot that God's Child was all around me. I was listening to the ego more and more and believing what I saw with my eyes, and I forgot that I could tune into the Holy Spirit on my own....

Worthiness

DavidPaul: Holy Spirit, what are some of the common barriers to hearing God's Voice?

Holy Spirit: "For so many, a barrier to God is a basic bottom line thought and belief that one is not worthy of God and God's Love. The thoughts can include that one is not good enough for God to love, that one has been bad, one has sinned, one has thought unlovingly about God, one has been angry toward God, blamed God, judged God, and so on. All of these thoughts would cause them to see themselves as unworthy of a relationship with God. For many, they have been disappointed by love. They feel that God has let them down or God has disappointed them. God has hurt them and God has punished them. There can be the idea that any and every thing that goes 'wrong' in their life is God's fault, God's doing, God's meanness, or God's wrath.

"There is the idea that when one is sick or hurt they have somehow done something wrong or disappointed God and are being punished. The illness or injury is proof that they are being punished by God, proof that they are not loved or worthy. The ego will seek proof everywhere. To the ego, an illness, an injury, a divorce, the death of a child or loved one, is all proof that God doesn't love them.

"Everything that happens can be seen from whatever perspective you choose. There are some who will look at things positively, some negatively, some with the idea that what is happening is proof of either God's Love or God's punishment. If one believes that God doesn't love them or they're not worthy of God, then their whole life will become proof of that. Rather than living a happy life, they will prove their point. Many would rather be right than happy. That again is the power of the ego."

Religion

Holy Spirit: "In asking what the barriers are to hearing God or connecting with God, some would think that they do not need God. Some do not want to be dependent on someone or something. Others do not believe that God exists. Some do not understand the system of God, so they don't bother with it."

DavidPaul: What do you mean by system?

Holy Spirit: "Either you pray and you love God, or you don't and you're punished. God will give you things if you pray in this way, and God won't if you don't. You must go to church at these times on these days and eat these things at these times and so on. It is so convoluted and so confusing for some that they would rather not bother because they don't understand the whole system. The system might mean religion or it might mean anything else.

"For many, what would keep them from God is religion. Ironically, religion could be one of the greater barriers to God. There are many beliefs, or dogma, that cause people to feel unworthy and failing in their relationship with God. There are many expectations and perfect concepts of how to have a relationship with God and how to experience God. One must speak in tongues on this particular day while they're spinning around three times and doing whatever else they are told. It is so difficult to reach the examples set for them or the rules established for them that many would run screaming from various religions in the world."

Perfection

Holy Spirit: "One of the most common barriers is the misunderstanding about perfection. For so many they don't understand that everything *is* perfect. They don't understand that when something happens, it is ultimately for the right reason. The original purpose of the world was to validate your separation from God, to make a place where God could not go so that you could have your autonomy. With Right-Mindedness, the world can serve another purpose as well. The world can be an opportunity to be reminded of who you are. With Right-Mindedness, the function of the world can serve a very high purpose indeed, and once you have been restored to the Truth of who you are, you will no longer need the world and it will fall away.

"In the meantime, with Right-Mindedness, everything that happens in the world *is* perfection. With Right-Mindedness, you are able to perceive everything that is happening either through eyes of love, so that you do not judge, or if you do judge, with ears of love so that you can perceive the Truth of a situation rather than the illusion.

"It is so easy for people to be confused and to believe that when something bad happens, it is because they are bad, they are not loved, God doesn't love them, they've done something wrong, or they are being punished, rather than to try over time to see what good might possibly come of it.

"Obviously, when one loses a child, you would not turn to them and say, 'Try to see the positive.' But over time, it may come to pass that those parents or siblings or grandparents or friends and family members might be able to appreciate the time that they had with that child, appreciate all that they received from that child, appreciate all the joy, experiences, and laughter that they would never have experienced otherwise. They may be grateful for what they did have, be grateful for the gift of that child in the world and have faith that for whatever reason that child's time in the world is complete. There may be other good things that come out of it, such as when a parent lobbies for laws to change or for conditions to shift around particular things involving children based on what happened to their child.

"It is so easy to blame and be victimized and suffer through what happens in the world and in life rather than to see the other side of it. With Right-Mindedness, whatever is happening in the world is serving you in the goal of remembering the Truth of who you are. No matter what happens, it is exactly the right thing to serve you to that end. You can have faith and trust that whatever is happening is exactly as it should be to give you your goal of returning to God. You have made the world as the perfect reminder and the perfect pathway Home if you have the right perspective."

––––––––––

DavidPaul: Perfection is an easy concept to understand from a distance or when things are going as we would like, but when we wish things were different, it's another matter altogether. Over the years, we too have struggled with making this concept real in our lives, especially in our relationship. Consequently, the Holy Spirit sometimes reminds us that we chose one another to overcome our most challenging issues—this is a nice way of saying that we often bring out the worst in one another.

When we first started to apply the concept of perfection in our relationship, we would often use it as justification or defense for not acknowledging each others' feelings and needs. For example, if Candace became annoyed with how dirty the house had become and I didn't feel like dealing with her frustration and desire for a cleaner house, I might have flippantly said, "Must be perfect." This, of course, would lead to an eventful evening of passionate conversation.

While it is true that all things are perfect—the messy house, Candace's frustration, her desire for order, my judgment of her frustration and desire for order, my flippant comment, and the fight that ensued—thinking the concept that all things are perfect doesn't do us much good unless we know how to apply this concept to our lives, to our thoughts and emotions, and to every situation that comes to us. *Chapter 8—Overcoming the Barriers to Hearing God Voice* will address how to do this.

Fear and Guilt

Holy Spirit: "If fear does indeed boil down to the possibility of losing what you have or not getting what you want, then people are frustrated by the idea that they cannot manipulate and control God for their own use. For example, someone will pray for something in the hope that they will get it. You *can* pray simply to talk with God, have connection and communion with God and your own sense of feeling good as a result of joining with God, or you can pray because you think you should, because you want something, you need something, or you've been told it is the thing to do. One will pray in the hope of getting on God's good side, and just that intention alone is a barrier. While one is praying, they are simultaneously building a barrier between themselves and God because of their intention and motivation for praying

"When one lives in the world, rather than with God, the belief that they are their body and that the body can live or die causes one to feel vulnerable and dependant upon God for God's mercy and grace. Fear and resentment on this dependence can build. To think that your well-being is based on God's kindness is a scary thought. You then must do whatever it is you think you must do to stay in God's good grace so that your body may be spared from some illness or accident.

"Some feel guilty that they seek God only in their time of need. When they are feeling desperate and on their knees, and they have the thought, 'I only seek God in my hour of need. I haven't been thankful for anything. I haven't been grateful. I haven't connected with God for any other reason,' then they get up off their knees and walk away from that possible joining because of guilt. The thought is that they would have to pray more consistently in order to receive God's Goodness in their time of need. In that same situation, they might be there on their knees not having joined with God in a very long time and feeling that it's been so long that God doesn't care about them or that God doesn't remember them because they haven't prayed enough and haven't been in union with God enough so they just aren't deserving of God. So even if they pray and even if God is right there with them, holding them, rocking them, and loving them, they can't experience it because they don't believe they deserve it.

"It's true that it doesn't matter what you think about God. If you don't believe in God, if you don't like God, if you don't understand God, if you don't care about God, that has nothing to do with God. And in fact, it has nothing to do with God's relationship with you. Just as someone can be in love with you and you don't have feelings for them, it is the same. God is in love with you and it doesn't matter how you feel about God; it doesn't change God's experience one bit. It is easy to think that you don't love God, therefore God doesn't love you. That couldn't be further from the Truth. It is easy to think you don't know or understand God, therefore, how could God know or understand you. Again, that is not true.

"It is only our projections onto God that allow us to experience God in whatever ways we do. Those are based on our thoughts about ourselves. When you are not liking you very much, it is very difficult to have a mutually rewarding, loving relationship with God. When you love and care about you, it is much easier to see that God loves and cares about you. When you judge you, when you don't accept you, it is very difficult to imagine that God can accept you unconditionally.

"Even when one understands what keeps them from the type of union with God that they truly seek in their heart, it doesn't mean that the thoughts won't pop up and keep you from your joining with God. But when you notice what you're thinking, 'Hmmm, I had a thought that I haven't been connecting with God frequently enough,' you can ask yourself, 'Is that true? Does God care? I'm here with God now and there is no time and space. This is the only moment there is and here I am with God. Thank you, God, for being here always for me to join with. Thank you for receiving me in this and all moments.' Then you can have your time and union with God.

"When you are able to notice that you are having a thought that is distracting you away from God, recognize that it is just a thought. It's not true now, nor has it ever been. The only Truth is that you are one with God, that God loves you just as you are and is completely aware of your Perfection that has never changed. Any thought you have that would take you away from God couldn't be true; it's just not possible. Acknowledge it for what it is. Let it go, and rejoin with God. Sit back down on God's Lap, settle in, get comfy, and feel God's Arms around you. Just lean back and enjoy it.

"There is the idea that only people who have studied religion for many, many years could ever be worthy of actually hearing God. So many people have the belief that only the Pope might receive some direct communication from God, only one who is more deserving, more sin free can hear. Neale Donald Walsch is one person who openly admits to hearing God and shares his conversations with God in books. He might be considered an example of the idea that if he can do it, anybody can. And the Truth is, everyone can and does.

"Some have experienced fear when hearing things and haven't trusted what they heard. Some have heard things that were frightening or that didn't make sense, so they stopped hearing. Some may have heard a grandparent who has passed on whisper something in their ear and it frightened them. It may have been a very sweet and loving communication, but it was frightening nonetheless. One may have heard God communicating to them as a child or in some other situation, and again it was just a frightening experience because it was unfamiliar, so one stops their ability to hear. It is as if they turn that off somehow.

"There are many who are fearful of what they might hear. They have heard that someone went out and murdered 68 people because God told them to. There are some who are afraid that if they hear God's Voice, they may be told something like that. For some, they may have tried and didn't hear and then became invalidated and gave up. There are some who have tried and tried and tried and tried and tried and tried and tried and tried, and they may even be hearing God, and they just don't realize it because they're trying so hard to hear It a certain way. They are so frustrated with the whole experience that their frustration is distracting them away from God's Voice.

"There are some who believe that to hear God you must follow a certain set of rules, or there might be only one established pathway for hearing God and they're not on it. Or there may be one incident in their past that they can't let go of, and when they sit down to talk to God, that is what is at the forefront of their mind and they are not able to hear. For some, there is just enough chatter, unfinished conversations, and thoughts floating around in one's head that there's actually too much noise to hear God talking. For many people, sitting alone, being still, focusing on breathing, quieting the mind, and letting go of all of the things that have to be done is very difficult.

"Again, there are 6 billion barriers to hearing God. These are a few."

DavidPaul's Story Continued

DavidPaul: While Candace and I were still living in Hawaii, my humbling experience trying to will myself into enlightenment once and for all brought me to the realization that I had no idea how to get myself out of the hole I had so willfully dug. I didn't actually understand why I was feeling so lifeless, nor did I know how to breathe any life back into me.

It was during this time of feeling so incredibly stuck that Candace started hearing the Holy Spirit on the Big Island. Feeling as if I had nowhere else to turn, I visited her to see if somehow the Holy Spirit could bring me back to life. We spent the entire weekend in a flurry of activity, swimming with dolphins, touring the island, visiting the volcano. Before we knew it, Candace was driving me back to the airport. She had wanted to give me communication from the Holy Spirit, but there was literally no time to do it.

We arrived at the airport thirty minutes early and sat down on a small patch of grass to wait for my plane's boarding call. As we did, Candace closed her eyes and began to speak—it was the first time I had ever heard Candace share the Words of the Holy Spirit. Sitting there on the grass, the Holy Spirit began to talk with me about "desire" and the opportunity to embrace it with love and acceptance rather than judgment. Since landing on Kauai, I had slowly and methodically judged and eradicated every thought that arose within me, including my desires—my desire to play, explore, learn, meet people, interact, and be in the world. I destroyed them all, banished them from my mind to try to maintain my awareness of Truth, at least I thought I banished them. In reality, I buried them under layers of judgment not knowing how else to integrate my experience of Truth into the world.

As the Holy Spirit spoke to me about my desires, I was lead out of the misery I made with my judgmental thinking and into an experience of embracing the desires within me in such a way that I no longer saw them as something to push away or avoid but as beautiful thoughts to embrace. In one magical moment listening to the Holy Spirit, the incessant and unconscious judgments that I had been harboring toward my desires suddenly fell away. What was left was an all-consuming passion within me to fully embrace those desires as a friend, to fully accept and allow my desires to exist without judgment. It was the first of many life changing experiences hearing the Holy Spirit.

I missed my plane, but it was worth it....

Thought

DavidPaul: How do our thoughts form our reality?

Holy Spirit: "Thought is the most powerful form of creation in the world. What one thinks, they may come to believe. What one believes, they may come to make real in the world. And it is the thought that one attaches to which becomes real, that then shapes the world and the way one sees it.

"Everything is a thought. Your concept of yourself is a thought. Your concept of your partner is a thought, which may be a whole large number of thoughts all put together to form this person who you perceive as your partner. Your home, your family, your job, the world, and everyone and everything in it are thoughts; and on top of those, you then have thoughts you think about everyone and everything in the world.

"Thoughts come and thoughts go. They mostly keep moving. Then one will arise, and it will be as if you have latched onto it, attached to that thought, and then that thought becomes real. Rather than just a concept floating by, it now begins to take on meaning. And with the meaning that you give that thought, it then begins to become a belief, which means with the way you experience that thought and the power you give it, you now have certain rules and experiences attached to that thought, which forms the world as you know it.

"Let's say, for example, that you have the belief that you *are* a body. Another might have the belief that they are a spirit who *has* a body. Then, on top of that belief, there is the belief that the body gets hungry. Then on top of that, there is the belief that the body needs food and water to survive. Then there is the belief that certain foods are good and certain foods are not; certain foods cause you to feel this way and certain foods do not; some may generate health, while others in your belief system may cause you to become ill; certain foods may be fattening and some may be energizing; and so on.

"All of these are thoughts that you have attached to that you now believe are true about you. And even though there are studies that prove that a certain food is good for you or bad for you, that study is a thought as well, or a belief if you attach to it. Whether or not you know what really happened in that study or the people and circumstances surrounding it, whether you heard a statistic or a quoted fact, now you believe that almonds are good for you and you eat almonds. You may or may not perceive a benefit in the body, and then you hear of another study that says that almonds are fattening or that many people are allergic to them or that in some way they are not beneficial, so you stop eating them. You do not know if anything you have been told about almonds is true. You just believe it, and then apply that belief to your body, which is just a thought as well. This is one tiny, tiny example of one's whole experience of living in the world.

"This is true of your experience of God as well. All of the thoughts that one has about God are what makes their reality of God. If you believe God is loving, then your God is loving. If you believe that God is angry and vengeful, then your God is angry and vengeful. The mind thinks thoughts and the ego attaches to those thoughts, gives them meaning, invents belief systems, and then manifests a world based on those thoughts and belief systems. The Holy Spirit, on the other hand, corrects the perception of the thought so that you see the Truth, which is ultimately that the thought itself is not true, therefore everything associated with that thought is not true either.

"In Reality, you are not the body and the body does not exist. You might think, 'Hmm, I am not the body. I am a spirit living in a body.' Then, you may go one step further and think, 'Hmm, bodies are something I dreamed up, to walk me through the world I dreamed up.'

"The Holy Spirit's job is to show you that, in fact, the body isn't real and every belief associated with the body, therefore, cannot be real. So as you begin to undo this house of cards, which are the beliefs you have surrounding the body, and as it all comes crashing down, you can begin to have the experience that, in fact, you don't have a body—or at least you cannot know if you have a body. You cannot know then if it needs to eat. You cannot know what is good for it and what isn't. At that point, all you can do is follow your heart. And when you have the thought to get up and prepare some food for you body, you just get up and prepare the food and eat it, and there are no thoughts associated with what is right or wrong for you. And it is one step closer to stepping out of the world and waking up from the dream."

Exercise—Thought vs. Reality

Holy Spirit: "Begin to become aware of your thoughts so that you can understand how you are affected by what you think, even though most of what you think may not be true. For example, when you wake up in the morning, you may have a thought about how much sleep you did or did not get and how that is going to impact your day. Or you may look out the window and have a thought about the weather and what that is going to mean. Or you might begin thinking about everything that you need to do that day. As a result, you are already in the future, rather than in this moment of waking up and welcoming a new day, connecting with yourself, Truth, or the Holy Spirit and just being thankful for a new day.

"You might begin thinking about what you are going to have for breakfast, whether or not you need a shower, what you are going to wear, and all of the things that you need to get done once you get up—the phone calls that must be made, a card that needs to be sent, something to be purchased along with all the work that has to get done. Before you know it, you are overwhelmed, exhausted, and sad or frustrated at all that you have to do, when the reality is, you are just lying in bed, yawning, stretching, and coming alive.

"Once you become aware of your thoughts, you can then notice the reality that you can give thanks for a new day, connect with yourself, connect with God, and appreciate what *is* in that moment. As the thoughts of the day begin to creep in, you can remind yourself of what you have to do in this moment—breathe, stretch, perhaps get out of bed, maybe stand up and put one foot in front of the other, but do not overwhelm yourself with just your thinking. Notice how often this occurs during the day and remind yourself that it is just a thought. Remind yourself of what your reality truly is in that moment. You are lying in bed, waking up, or you are just picking up peaches at the store. You have no worries, no fears, no suffering, and you can enjoy each moment that you are able to remember that."

Chapter Highlights

"Everything that happens can be seen from whatever perspective you choose."

"One of the most common barriers is the misunderstanding about perfection. For so many they don't understand that everything *is* perfect. They don't understand that when something happens, it is ultimately for the right reason."

"When you are able to notice that you are having a thought that is distracting you away from God, recognize that it is just a thought. It's not true now, nor has it ever been…. Acknowledge it for what it is. Let it go, and rejoin with God."

"Thought is the most powerful form of creation in the world. What one thinks, they may come to believe. What one believes, they may come to make real in the world. And it is the thought that one attaches to which becomes real, that then shapes the world and the way one sees it."

8

Overcoming the Barriers to Hearing God's Voice

"There is no difference between love and healing.
They are one and the same.
They are each accomplished by the other in the mind."

Holy Spirit: "There are a wide variety of thoughts that keep one from hearing God's Voice, and yet, they are all just thoughts. Because thoughts are so powerful, they each seem to take on a power of their own and each seem to mean something different that must be overcome or understood or solved. But a thought is just a thought, regardless of the meaning you give it, and every thought that keeps you from hearing Truth has an opposite thought that can open the door to Truth. Therefore, it is very simple to overcome the barriers to hearing God because those barriers are just a thought and you can choose to think differently. The challenge is in noticing that you are having a thought that does not serve you. It has become so comfortable and familiar to think thoughts that take you away from the Truth…that noticing them is now the difficulty.

"With awareness, intention, practice, and determination, you can become aware of what you are thinking and make a decision about what you want to think. The more you do it, the easier it becomes—until one day, it is just a way of life."

Self-Awareness

DavidPaul: "Holy Spirit, how can one overcome the barriers to hearing God's Voice?"

Holy Spirit: "To overcome the barriers to hearing God, you must first recognize that what you are hearing is not God and you must have the desire to hear God. At some point, the noise of the world becomes so shrill, loud, and invasive that one becomes aware that they are not enjoying what they are hearing and perhaps there might be a better way.

"It is easy to forget about God and to be distracted by the pace and the temptations of the world. There is a very deep part of you that is nagging you to remember that, in fact, this is just a dream. A sincere desire to connect with God and God's Voice will ultimately take you there. In Truth, that is all you could desire because that is the Truth of who you are and the Truth of your heritage. Since you have never been separate, that is all you seek to remember.

"Take notice of your life. Take notice of your body, your health, anything within your body that is not effortless and pain-free. Take notice of your home and your family, your work, your finances, your part in society. Then take note of you and how you feel on a day-to-day basis. You may have everything that the world says you should have to be happy, and yet you may not be happy. Or you may have everything and think you are happy, yet you find yourself angry much of the time. You may have few of the things the world says you need to be happy and you may be resentful about that or sad about that. Your health may be seriously compromised, or you may be holding thoughts all day of attack, blame, and judgment.

"How you feel and how you think are the keys to how you are really doing. If your mind is happy, if you are at peace, if you are contented with your life, accepting of your neighbor, understanding of yourself and your family, loving what is, then you know that you have a strong foothold in Reality, which is not of this world. If in fact you are unhappy, depressed, sad, angry, resentful, or guilty, or if you are judging your neighbors, resenting your family, judging the world, or wishing that things were different, then you can be assured that your mind is not with God. You are not in Right-Mindedness.

"If you are on a continual quest for more, more money—more stuff, more time, more love, more joy—that is a sign to you that your thinking is not working for you and that, in Truth, what you are seeking is more connection with God. You can go out in pursuit of more of this and that for the rest of your life and what you are ultimately seeking is more of a connection with God. Once you become aware of that, you stop, you sit, and you say hello to God and you connect with God and it happens in that instant. You know there are barriers between you and God any time you are not happy, fulfilled, contented, at peace, or accepting and understanding of all things. It is the awareness and understanding that if all things are not at peace in your life, then it is time to stop and connect.

"Once you become aware that your thinking is a barrier to God, it can be very easy to restore your mind to Truth in the sense that awareness is a huge piece of the puzzle. Once you become aware that your thinking is not working for you, then you can begin the search for Right-Thinking."

Self-Inquiry

Holy Spirit: "As you become more aware of your thoughts, you become aware of your beliefs. As you begin to question these beliefs, knowing that nothing in the world is True or Real, you can begin to let them go and shed the beliefs that have weighed you down for so long and kept you from your communication with God. You begin to question the belief that you hadn't realized caused you pain and you come to understand that maybe what you have always thought isn't in fact true, and one chain is removed from you that has been tying you down.

"You become aware of another belief…something as simple as boys think this way, or feel this way, or act this way to something as complicated as death is forever or death is final. As you begin to question these beliefs, you release the chains that have kept you bound and you become more free of the world each time. The more free of the world you become, the more opportunity for God to take the place of those beliefs—God being Love or Truth or Reality.

"In asking, 'Is it true that winter is cold and lonely and depressing?' you may come to find that, in fact, winter may become the same as any other season or you may come to find many gifts and miracles in winter or you may come to use it as an opportunity to go within, to hibernate as a bear might, to let go of a belief or to change a belief so that it serves you and gives you a tremendous sense of freedom. Eventually, the more you question your thoughts about winter, the more you will come to understand that winter is just a thought. It doesn't even exist, and every day will be the same, but from a place of Truth or Reality, that whatever is in front of you is perfect. You do not judge or evaluate what is in front of you. It just is. You may get to a point of not labeling what is in front of you and ultimately just being present, experiencing love, true understanding, true acceptance, and the peace and joy that come with that.

"It is a freedom from the world that the deepest part of you seeks, knowing that in overcoming the world, all that is left is God, which is all there ever has been, all there ever will be. You have just forgotten. As you overcome the world and your Oneness is remembered and restored, the ego is forgotten. It is as if it never existed, because in Truth, it never did, right along with the world, and you are left to revel in your Wholeness, your Completeness, your Oneness with all that is, without question, just Joy."

Candace: Because the Holy Spirit works with our mind as well as God's, the Holy Spirit will bring through what is in my mind—phrases, experiences, thoughts, and expressions that are somewhat uniquely mine. After spending a number of years doing "The Work of Byron Katie," which is the process of writing down our judgments, questioning them, and then "turning them around" so they can be seen from a different perspective, when I hear the Holy Spirit or share the Words of the Holy Spirit, sometimes an aspect of "The Work" will come through.

The Work, which I discovered at the same time that I began hearing God's Voice, has been a very powerful process in my life. I have used the Work to undo my beliefs about my family, my body, my relationships, and my life, and have gained tremendous freedom in all of those areas from understanding the Truth of my thinking. Like the Holy Spirit, the Work is a process that has the ability to take one to Right-Mindedness.

Exercise—The Truth of the Holy Spirit

Holy Spirit: "If you have doubts or fears about your ability to hear God's Voice, make a list of those doubts and fears. It might include:

1. The Holy Spirit isn't real.

2. I will never hear the Holy Spirit.

3. The Holy Spirit is not inside of me.

4. I am not worthy of hearing the Holy Spirit.

5. God doesn't love me so I don't have the Holy Spirit.

6. And so on....

"Then, with each one of these beliefs, begin to question whether or not you can really know if that is true. Can you really know that the Holy Spirit is not real? Can you really know that you won't be able to hear the Holy Spirit? Can you know definitively that you are not worthy of God, God's Voice, or God's Love?

"As you ask yourself these questions, you may come to realize that you cannot know if these thoughts are true or not. Begin to open your mind to the possibility that, in fact, you might be wrong. Begin to open your mind to the possibility that the Holy Spirit *does* exist, you *will* hear God's Voice, that in fact, you *do* hear God's Voice, that you *are* worthy of God and God's Love, and that the Holy Spirit *is* within you, and focus on these possibilities rather than the others.

"It's just as likely that these are true and, in fact, much more likely. You may as well put your faith into that which is hopeful and enjoyable to believe, knowing ultimately that it has to be true because, in Reality, only God, God's Child, and God's Voice exist."

All Paths Lead to God

DavidPaul: Self awareness and self inquiry are simple practices, but they are not necessarily easy. The ego is amazingly good at its job. As a result, countless practices have been designed with the intention to heal our minds, experience Truth, understand ourselves, undo our beliefs, overcome the ego, and be in the present moment. These practices range from a wide variety of meditation and self awareness methods to physical disciplines such as yoga, tai chi, and many others. Support groups, spiritual and religious organizations, prayer, professional counseling, talking with friends and family, reading spiritual or self-help books, and following our hearts and dreams are but a few of the things we can do that also have the potential to help bring awareness to our minds.

The list of methods and techniques for overcoming the ego is far-reaching. Ultimately, all methods that restore God's Children to Right-Mindedness are a blessing, and the Holy Spirit will work through anything to accomplish this. Because restoring our minds to Right-Thinking *is* the function of the Holy Spirit, we can also join directly with the Holy Spirit as a way of undoing the thoughts and beliefs that would keep us from having the relationship with God and ourselves we truly long for.

Using the Holy Spirit

DavidPaul: Holy Spirit, how can one use this Voice to overcome the barriers to hearing this Voice within them?

Holy Spirit: "Since God has given everyone His Voice inside of them, that of the Holy Spirit, it is then equally possible for all of God's children to connect with Truth and Right-Mindedness through the Holy Spirit. God gave His Children an Interpreter, one who could see all sides of things, understand the temptations of the ego versus the Truth in ways that God does not comprehend or cannot talk to you about because God does not perceive the ego. There are no restorations to make from God's perspective. There is just connection and Oneness.

"Restoring yourself to Right-Mindedness can happen instantly as you connect with God through your own doing, or it can happen through the work of the Holy Spirit by asking the Holy Spirit to help restore your mind to Right-Thinking. You can ask the Holy Spirit to be with you, share with you a perspective of Truth to guide you, direct you, and comfort you in the ways of Reality rather than illusion. You can ask the Holy Spirit to hold your hand and give you that which you need to maneuver your way around the world as you make your way to God.

"In Truth, you can use Jesus in the same way. You can ask Jesus to be with you, to help you restore your mind to Right-Thinking, to hold your hand as you walk through the world, afraid but growing in Faith, with the desire for your Oneness to be restored to you. What Jesus learned in his lifetime as Jesus was to think only with the thinking of the Holy Spirit, rather than with the thinking of the ego. In that way, Jesus overcame the world and is here in your heart and mind to mentor you in that same way as well. Jesus has been the example of what that looks like in an earthly form so that you can come to know it is possible to hear only God's Voice through the Holy Spirit. If you are hearing God's Voice, you cannot hear the ego. If you hear the ego, you cannot hear God's Voice at the same time—they do not talk over each other.

"The ego does not get destroyed in this process of hearing God's Voice; it just becomes dormant. You can hear the Holy Spirit at all times if that is what you seek. You can have that be the only Voice you hear. That does not mean you have annihilated the ego in the process. It means you choose, in every moment, the Holy Spirit, the Voice for Truth, the Comforter, the Call to Joy, and the ego soon becomes a quiet and powerless voice in the back of your mind."

Befriending Our Thoughts

DavidPaul: Holy Spirit, I often find myself judging my thoughts. How can I relate to them in a way that serves me?

Holy Spirit: "Thoughts themselves are not the enemies. It is only what we do with a thought that can harm us. You can ignore a thought, question a thought, believe a thought, act on a thought…. All of those are up to you. The thoughts come. That is the mind's job. What you do with them is your choice.

"The thoughts are innocent in and of themselves and have no power, no meaning, and no impact. It is what you do with a thought that gives it meaning. If you have a thought that you like, you can hold on to that thought. You can believe it. You can act on it and enjoy what you get from it. If you have a thought that you do not like, you need not be a victim to it, but rather you can question it. Is that thought true? Can you really know that whatever it is you are thinking is true? And if it does not serve you to keep that thought, then let it go.

"As one begins to work on their mind or master their thinking, they may perceive all of their thoughts as enemies. The truth is, thought creates. You were created from a Thought of God, and everything in your world was made from a thought. Rather than presuming that every thought you have is the enemy or will distract you from Truth or is somehow keeping you from that which you truly seek, you can instead meet every thought as an innocent friend.

"If you have a thought that you do not like for whatever reason, you can thank the thought for existing and allow it to go on its way. It is not bad just because *you* don't like it. Another person may have the same thought and enjoy it, keep it, believe it, and act on it. Thoughts are not inherently good or bad. That is determined by the meaning you give them. Presuming they are all innocent, you meet them and greet them, and you keep the ones you like and you let go of the ones you do not, not from a place of anger, purging, or fear, but from a place of cleaning out, just as you would clean out your cupboards in the spring. It is not because something is good or bad that you would get rid of it. It is because it no longer serves a purpose for you and you let it go. You make room for new things that you like more.

"This is easily accomplished from a place of Right-Mindedness, but even without that, you can still sit patiently and lovingly, and as each thought comes to you, greet it, welcome it, examine it, and then kindly keep it or let it go. There is no fear in this. There is no urgency. And there is no anger or hatred. There is acceptance, understanding, love, and peace, and that is what you would seek in any situation. Apply it to your thoughts, and you will watch it manifest in your life in amazing and wonderful ways."

DavidPaul's Story Continued

DavidPaul: After the life changing communication I received from the Holy Spirit about embracing my desires at the Kona airport, I stepped off the plane on Kauai full of passion and life once again. I went from an apathetic, lifeless man to one on a mission to embrace his desires. While I won't go into unnecessary details, having nearly withered away to a mere 110 pounds upon my arrival at Candace's doorstep, food and my joyful and gluttonous embracing of it soon become a wonderful pastime.

Since my new goal in life was to fully embrace my desires as completely as possible, I went to Foodland one night after work and bought 16 double packages of Reece's peanut butter cups. I went home, meditated a bit, and then proceeded to slowly and consciously savor each delicious cup as if it was the only thing that existed in the world. It took me two hours to consume all 32 cups, not because I was full or because they were making me sick, but because I was completely joining with every ounce of flavor and experience I could allow myself to feel. It was absolutely stupendous.

The following week, I performed the same ritual with Ben & Jerry's Chocolate Fudge Brownie ice cream, this time slowly devouring 3 pints in one glorious sitting. By fully embracing my desires with unconditional love and acceptance, I came to notice that my desires rarely returned. To this day, I have no desire for candy bars or ice cream, not because I ate too much of them, but because I fully experienced those desires within me. I haven't purchased a candy bar or eaten ice cream ever since. For better or worse, or neither, the desire to do so just doesn't exist.

After several months of enjoying my gluttony and living out every desire I truly wanted, my passion and joy began to plateau, and I started getting restless. I immediately recognized the warning signs and called Candace to ask for communication from the Holy Spirit. Much to my surprise, the communication I received was similar to what I received before, but instead of talking about desire, the Holy Spirit spoke about feeling my emotions. It was the same theme—loving and embracing my emotions without judgment.

For much of my life, I viewed emotion as something to either overcome or express. As soon as I became aware of an emotion, I would immediately judge its value. Do I get rid of it? Or do I take a stand? If the answer was getting rid of it, I typically stuffed it or willed myself out of having it. If the emotion seemed honorable, justifiable, or worth fighting for, I'd throw on my armor and go to battle, either subtly or not so subtly. Either way I chose, peace and freedom still eluded me.

As I listened to the Words of the Holy Spirit over the phone with Candace, the unconscious judgments I had been harboring toward my emotions were immediately released. What was left was a bounding sense of joy and passion. During the communication, the Holy Spirit led me through an exercise of feeling my emotions. I then practiced this exercise each day for several months.

First, I would close my eyes and find a safe and secure connection to Truth within me. Anchored in this connection, I would then imagine a water faucet in front of me. As I turned the valve, my emotions would begin to flow through me. Maintaining my connection with Truth and Right-Mindedness, I would then allow myself to embrace the emotions that came. Very similar to the exercise of eating peanut butter cups and ice cream, I would feel, with all of my attention, every emotion that arose—fear, anger, hatred, sadness…often sobbing for long periods of time throughout the exercise.

Being anchored in Right-Mindedness while simultaneously feeling my emotions allowed me to witness the rising and falling of my emotions without judgment. While I assume they were connected to or the result of some triggering thought or perception, instead of focusing on the cause of the emotion, I just felt them. If I noticed myself identifying, judging, trying to understand, evaluate, or do anything but feel the emotions that arose within me, I would immediately return my attention to *only* feeling. That was my goal and only focus.

At first, it was frightening to feel my emotions so strongly. Tears would often stream down my face for twenty or thirty minutes straight. Then, the tears would stop and into me would flow a deep sense of peace and joy. It was an intense practice, and yet the cycle was always the same, intense emotion followed by incredible peace. When I was ready, I would open my eyes, get up, and go about my day feeling refreshed, alive, and on top of the world.

After several months, the idea of lovingly embracing my desires and emotions without judgment began to spread and I started to see the possibility of embracing every thought with the same intention and perspective. As this possibility took root, I began to lose the distinction between my inner thoughts, emotions, and beliefs and those seemingly outside of me, like my body, another person, or a physical thing or event in the world. From my perspective, they were all equal. They were all a thought in one form or another, and I could apply this practice to all of them.

Eventually, as my desire to embrace and experience all things without judgment began to blossom within me, I knew in my heart that my time in Hawaii had come to an end. I had given myself the gift of coming to understand how it is possible to live in Truth while simultaneously living in the illusion of the world. It was now time to apply this concept to every area of my life, every thought in my mind, and every moment of my day.

Little did I know how difficult that would be....

Play

DavidPaul: Holy Spirit, what about playing and having fun? Where do they fit into this?

Holy Spirit: "Play is just an acknowledgment to lighten up, to not take things so seriously. One can have their Oneness with God and still be incredibly serious and heavy. It is taken so seriously. Even with a certain sense of freedom from the world, there is still a life or death type of experience people bring to their relationship with God or to their spirituality.

"Play is an invitation simply to lighten up, to play as little children with God, and to play in the world. You came here truly to play. Yes, it is a school, but school is not about work. It is about growing, learning, exploring, investigating, making friends, and doing different things. And if that's the case, then lighten up and play and have some fun.

"There are kids who spend their day studying, learning, trying, in effort, doing homework, and doing extra projects. They could just have some fun and not take it so seriously. You learn what you need to learn, and you won't learn what you don't need to learn. Most of it is not True or Real anyway. Just try to have some fun and know that you will always learn what you need to learn.

"There is the idea for many that they need to prove to God their commitment, their dedication, or their loyalty, and this is done through seriousness. The one who serves Jesus is the one who sits at his feet and listens to him and connects with him, rather than the one who 'serves' him food or drink. The one who serves is also present with him, and in 'playing' with another in that way, it is a tremendous service. It is a tremendous way of being present with another, being in the moment, having this thought and going with it and having that thought and going with it.

"When one is playing, there are no problems. There are no fears. There are no worries. There is very little in the way of illusion and very much in the way of happiness, fulfillment, peace, and love."

The Temple of the Holy Spirit

DavidPaul: From all that I've heard and gained over the years in listening to the Voice of the Holy Spirit through Candace and myself, I've come to understand that all healing in the world—the healing of our thoughts, emotions, beliefs, physical ailments, relationships, and circumstances—is the result of creating a Holy Relationship within our heart and mind with whatever it is we appear to be "healing." For example, if one notices they are holding a thought or belief that is causing them pain or if one finds them self in a situation that is painful, instead of wanting it to change, trying to make it better, or pushing the thought or emotion aside because they do not like it or want it, they can instead create a relationship with that thought, emotion, or situation that is filled with acceptance, peace, love, compassion, and understanding. A Holy Relationship is when there is no judgment, no attack, no suppression, no wanting something to be different than it is. A Holy Relationship is when one perceives the thought or situation through the Eyes of the Holy Spirit. It is experiencing *all of it,* everything identifiable, with Right-Mindedness.

It is often said that if you are in pain or if you want something to be different, change it. As creative beings, we have this power. We have the power to manifest anything we want through our thinking. And yet, so often, we change things in our life, including our thoughts, beliefs, and circumstances, because we think the new thought or situation is somehow better…and now the old thought, belief, or circumstance that we have just moved on from is somehow wrong, inferior, or something to be avoided—not only wrong for ourselves but for everyone else as well. Often times, we feel better for having overcome these thoughts and beliefs.

We experience ourselves as having evolved or as having become more aligned with Truth, and yet we don't always recognize how we judge everyone else who has yet to make this change in *their* life.

Without creating a Holy Relationship with whatever it is we experience as painful—without that love, acceptance, and understanding in our heart and mind—the ego continues to reign. We are simply swapping one belief or thought for another. While it may seem that we would rather have this new perspective or situation than the previous, without a Holy Relationship, our pain still persists. It is just being masked by the new thought or belief that we now prefer, and everyone else who has yet to take this step with us is often seen as wrong, in pain, or simply not getting it.

Creating a Holy Relationship with our thoughts, feelings, and circumstances—truly loving *what is* without wanting it to be different—offers us the opportunity for true healing. The Holy Spirit once told Candace and me that the Temple of the Holy Spirit is not a body but a relationship. At the time, I thought the Holy Spirit was referring only to relationships between people because we first heard this communication when Candace and I initially got together. After years of hearing this Voice within me and learning how to apply It to my life, I now understand that the Holy Spirit was referring to our relationship with *all things,* not just with each other.

As the Holy Spirit once said through Jesus, "Where two or more are gathered in my name, there am I in the midst of them." While this is certainly true for our relationship with people, it is equally true for our relationship with every thought, belief, word, and deed that has ever been held by the split mind of God's Child.

Chapter Highlights

"To overcome the barriers to hearing God, you must first recognize that what you are hearing is not God and you must have the desire to hear God."

––––––––––

"As you overcome the world and your Oneness is remembered and restored, the ego is forgotten. It is as if it never existed, because in Truth, it never did, right along with the world, and you are left to revel in your Wholeness, your Completeness, your Oneness with all that is, without question, just Joy."

––––––––––

"If you are hearing God's Voice, you cannot hear the ego. If you hear the ego, you cannot hear God's Voice at the same time; they do not talk over each other."

––––––––––

"It is not because something is good or bad that you would get rid of it. It is because it no longer serves a purpose for you and you let it go. You make room for new things that you like more."

––––––––––

"When one is playing, there are no problems. There are no fears. There are no worries. There is very little in the way of illusion and very much in the way of happiness, fulfillment, peace, and love."

––––––––––

Without creating a holy relationship with whatever it is we experience as painful—without that love, acceptance, and understanding in our heart and mind—the ego continues to reign.

9

Prayer

"Prayer opens the door and God is waiting patiently
on the other side of that door,
at all times, in all situations, to join with you."

Holy Spirit: "It is easy to misunderstand prayer, how to use it, and its purpose and function while living in the world. Regardless of what one prays for, prayer has only one true function. Regardless of what one seeks, prayer can only be used in one way. It does not matter to whom you pray, how you pray, or why you pray, God is the only Source, and your prayer opens the door to Him."

What Is Prayer?

Candace: Holy Spirit, what is prayer and how can it be used to hear God's Voice?

Holy Spirit: "Prayer is one of the greatest tools one can have in the world because it opens the door to a dialogue with God. It is called prayer in the sense that you know to whom you are speaking, rather than the form that it takes. Prayer means that one is engaged in a dialogue with God in particular and/or God's Voice. Prayer means that you are beginning a dialogue with the One Who created you, the One who never left you, and you are reestablishing that connection within your mind, within your heart, and giving yourself the opportunity to have a deeper experience with Source. Prayer is the opportunity to transcend the world in any given moment and connect with what is really True and Real.

When one chooses prayer, one is choosing to step aside from all that seems to be happening and seek connection with their Father.

"If you say a prayer to God and you stop for a moment and connect with God, acknowledge God, thank God, or appreciate God in the course of that prayer, its function will have been fulfilled. If you say a prayer without acknowledging God or connecting with God in some way, then the function of the prayer is not fulfilled. It does not matter what is prayed for and it does not matter what the outcome of the specific request is because the function of the prayer is to connect with God, to remember Truth, to overcome the dream in that moment. This is not necessarily acknowledged or understood in the moment, but by asking something of One Whom you've never seen and have no proof of, just by that act, you are overcoming the world.

"If you say a prayer because you think you should, because it is the right thing to do, because it couldn't hurt, or out of an obligation or responsibility, again the prayer does not fulfill its function. A prayer can be as simple as 'Hello, God' or 'Thank You, God' or it can be an unending dialogue about anything you want to share with God. Prayer need not happen in a church, but only in the church within you. If you are walking down the street, driving in your car, or shopping in a store, and you have the thought to say hello to God, or thank God, or ask for something in as light-hearted and casual a way or as serious a way as you feel called, it is all the same.

"Many believe they must be serious and reverent in their prayers with God, and yet that is very unnecessary. Remembering God in any happy moment as well as a challenging moment is a wonderful blessing for everyone, and to connect with God in whatever place you are is always welcome.

"Prayer is necessary in the process of hearing God's Voice. It is not that you must get on your knees and pray the rosary this many times a day in these ways and then you will someday hear God. It is truly that prayer is what opens the dialogue. Prayer begins the conversation. One person has to start talking for another person to talk back. It does not matter who talks first, what is said, where, how, or anything else, though as long as two people sit silently, no dialogue will occur. It could be said that God talks to you at all times, and at some point, you acknowledge that and you talk back and that is prayer. Then you hear God more specifically because you are now engaged in the conversation. Once you begin that conversation through prayer, whatever that looks like, that relationship is begun.

"Obviously one can pray to many things, but the idea is always that prayer is directed toward Source or Creator. So whether one calls that the Sun, the Earth, Allah, Buddha, God, Jesus, or Christ, it doesn't matter. It is all being directed to the same Source, to the Creator of what is Real, and it is a way of asking to transcend the world.

"When one prays, they are opening the door to a communication with God and seeking a connection with what is Real. They are trying to get past their experience of the world, of the dream, and to remind themselves of what is True. Prayer is the opportunity to talk with God, and God hears all prayers. When one begins a dialogue with God, God listens. God hears all communication directed to Him, and God doesn't listen to communication that is not directed to Him. All of the chatter of the world goes ignored. It is just part of the dream. It isn't real. It has no meaning, and God doesn't listen to it. Though any communication directed toward Him is heard.

"When the mind split and the ego was invented, the Holy Spirit was the answer to that prayer and has been the answer to every prayer since. When one is afraid, they may pray for their physical safety, yet because this is a dream, what they really seek is the peace of knowing and remembering that this is just a dream and there is nothing to fear. Their prayer is answered immediately, though when the answer is *received* is up to the one who prayed."

――――――――

Candace: When I first started hearing the Voice of the Holy Spirit, It would come to me in meditation and throughout the day. Sometimes I would just put my attention on that Voice, and I would hear It. When my now husband sent me my first listener, I knew that I had to have a prayer to start the session with. I needed a way to call on the Holy Spirit and set an intention that what I would hear would be this Voice and no other. So I asked the Holy Spirit for a prayer, and though I still don't know exactly what it means, the prayer I heard was this:

"May it be with your blessings, God, that these words that come through are Yours, and only Yours. May they bring joy and light to those who hear them, and wisdom and knowledge to those who don't. Thank You, God. Amen."

Since that day, I've said this prayer every time I've ever shared this Voice. I also ask the Holy Spirit if It is willing to come through me. After more than ten years of asking, so far I've only heard three replies—"yes," "yes, of course," and "yes of course, precious one." I also ask if the Holy Spirit will help me get out of the way of the communication, and sometimes I ask, "May this be exactly what we all need to hear," though I know this last request isn't necessary.

I usually say the prayer I was given three times in my head before I feel that I am connected with every word of it and connected with God and the Holy Spirit. There have been times, however, when I've needed to say the prayer 20 or 30 times, and on a few rare occasions, when I've only said it once and felt connected. Sometimes I say the prayer out loud because I can't quiet my mind enough to connect with the Holy Spirit. When I do, I often start off by saying hello to God and the Holy Spirit. Other times, I put my index finger on my forehead to help me focus as I say the prayer to myself. I also try to remember to thank God for the opportunity to hear His Voice before the session or after.

This prayer is important to me because it puts me in a clear place with a clear intention. I also find that saying hello to God and asking the Holy Spirit if the Holy Spirit is willing to come through me feels like the right thing to do. Although I've come to understand that the Holy Spirit loves to have the opportunity to share Truth with me, my family, and anyone else who seeks It, I will continue to ask the Holy Spirit if It is willing to come through me every time. As long as I keep hearing yes, I will keep sharing this Voice.

Each person will find their own way to connect with this Voice, and it may or may not involve prayer. For myself, I find that some sort of consistent ritual is helpful—it is something I can count on. Sometimes, when I have been away from the Voice for awhile and I say that prayer and reconnect, it is very familiar and comforting and can help erase the time that has gone by.

Prayer for Worldly Things

Candace: Holy Spirit, what about praying for things in the world?

Holy Spirit: "The world is just a thought. If you say a prayer for something in the world, you are really ultimately asking your mind to manifest what you prayed for. God doesn't create that for you. The Holy Spirit doesn't create that for you. These types of prayers are not answered in the sense that the clouds part and God brings a house down into the world for you. It is that you have the thought of something you want and based on your thoughts, you will either manifest that or you won't. You will have the thought that you can have that or the thought that you can't, and based on that, you will manifest it or not. When one asks for a relationship or a job and does so in prayer, they are really making an intention about what it is they want and then ultimately working with their mind to get it.

"When one says a prayer, say for a relationship, and then sits and waits for that relationship to show up and they don't do anything but wait and keep asking God and wait some more and keep asking God, generally nothing happens. When one says a prayer for a relationship, they are declaring what they want and making an opening to move in that direction. They will then begin with their mind opening up to a relationship, contemplating what they want, and preparing themselves for it in a variety of ways. Again, based on their thinking, they will either manifest that relationship or they won't, and that has nothing to do with God. It is so easy to say, 'God doesn't give me what I want. God doesn't answer my prayers,' and to not take responsibility for what one manifests in the world.

"God's function is to see only your Perfection as you were created, to love you unconditionally, and to forever hold the Truth as what is Real. That has nothing to do with the world. It is not to say that it is pointless to pray for worldly things, only to be aware that the desire for prayer is ultimately the desire to connect with God. Wanting something badly enough to pray for it is part of the design for you to be so motivated as to connect and communicate with God. You think you want these worldly things so badly that you will pray and ask God for them, but they are just the means, not the end.

"Some people use prayer as proof that God loves them. Some people use prayer as proof that God doesn't. If one is able to manifest the big house that they have prayed for, then God loves them, and if they are not able to manifest it, then God doesn't. This is obviously the ego's game because eventually there will be something that you pray for that will not manifest, and all of the other answered prayers will become meaningless.

"If you want worldly things such as a family, a home, a job, good health, or whatever it may be, you can ask God to join you in your thinking to be able to manifest what is best for you. Ask God to join you in your thinking so that you can perceive the world, what's in it, and your path in such a way as to have whatever peace, connection, and comfort you desire. You can ask the Holy Spirit to work with you and your mind to help you see the Truth of any situation so that you can know better what to ask for, how to ask for it, and how to move in that direction. Having worldly or earthly goals is not the problem. It is understanding how they manifest and your part in it that is confusing and can be invalidating or disruptive in your relationship with God."

DavidPaul's Story Continued

DavidPaul: I left Hawaii with the dream of fully embracing all that life had to offer. What better way to do that, I thought, than to travel the world? So I purchased a one-way ticket around the globe with the hope of somehow returning the master of it. I knew what to do and how to do it. How difficult could it be to experience the world without judgment?

Six months later, I stepped off the plane in San Francisco a bit disillusioned that I had not come back completely transformed or in any way more enlightened than when I had left. Living on my friend's couch in Oakland without a dime to my name, I became acutely aware that experiencing Truth in the world was not something I was going to check off my to-do-list and be done with. It was going to be a moment to moment, day-to-day process that would unfold for the rest of my life.

With this new, sobering outlook on life, I set out to get a "real job" for the first time in my life. If all things were truly equal, I thought, why not do what everyone else was doing? So I decided to get a job in high-tech. Within a few months, I landed a job at 3Com doing tech-support, and in no time at all, I was back on my feet. I had an apartment, a car, and a whole new life.... The only thing I was missing was someone to share it with.

I had never thought about marriage in my entire life, but as time went on, the desire for companionship, intimacy, and union with another human being began to grow within me. One night while I was sleeping, I had a dream that would change the course of my life. In the dream, I was kneeling down on a small boat in the middle of the ocean. Candace stood in front of me wearing a long, white dress. As I looked up at her, a wave of intense fear came over me. I could hardly breathe or speak. I struggled to open my mouth, and as I did, I suddenly woke up.

Completely stunned, I immediately sat up in bed, closed my eyes, and visualized being back in the dream. I felt the fear that had gripped me so strongly, and as it began to melt away, a deep and abiding love for Candace flowed into me, a love for her that I had never felt before. I spent several hours in meditation that night, joining with and feeling all of the thoughts and emotions that arose within me. I also sought guidance on what was in my highest good and how to deal with this new experience. By the time I was done, I knew that I loved Candace and wanted to have a life with her. There was only one problem—she was committed to someone else!

I agonized for days whether I should tell her. In the end, I realized that I only wanted her to be happy and did not want to ruin what she was making for herself, so I said, "God, if this is meant to be, it's in Your Hands. There's nothing I can do." I then took down her picture at work and stopped calling or e-mailing her altogether.

Six months later, she e-mailed me and said that she was leaving her boyfriend. My heart leapt. My adrenaline surged. I broke out in a sweat reading her e-mail! Six phone calls, six weeks, and one plane ticket later, she was on her way to California to begin a life with me....

Prayer for the Highest Good

Candace: Holy Spirit, what does it mean to ask for what is in one's highest good when seeking guidance, direction, or in prayer?

Holy Spirit: "When one is aware that they do not know what is the best outcome, when they do not know what is best for someone else or themselves, or when they do not know how something should unfold, though they may have beliefs or thoughts of how they would like it to unfold, one can simply pray for that which is in the highest good. In praying for the highest good in any situation, you can trust that whatever is truly the best for one's path will unfold. This can include a situation involving a loved one or your family, or it could be a war in another part of the world.

"Pray for that which is in the highest good of everyone involved and ask God to be with everyone in their thinking, so that if they choose, they may be able to perceive Right-Mindedness for a moment. The pattern in the world is to seek the path of least resistance. It is the norm for one to do that which is easiest, with the quickest results or most immediate gratification. Most advice and most solutions offer a short-term answer, rather than a long-term answer. When one asks for guidance involving a particular situation and asks for that which is in their highest good, that will not necessarily be the easiest, the quickest, or filled with the most immediate gratification, but rather may be a long-term solution.

"The simplest example is when one is in a relationship with someone and one party does not want to be in the relationship and one party does. The party who does is heartbroken and wants the other person to be with them. The easiest, simplest answer is to just convince this other person, who is already there, to continue with what they have been doing because it is good enough and because then that person who is heart broken will not have to experience pain, sadness, or loneliness.

"If one were in that situation and praying for guidance and asking for that which is in their highest good, they may hear why it is that they have been with that person, what it is they have been learning, what they have gained from that experience, and why now it is important to let it go. They may hear that ultimately there is a better situation for them at hand and that the relationship they are in has already fulfilled its purpose. It is complete for whatever reason. Just because someone is not complete with the situation has nothing to do with what is in their highest good. If they ask what is in their highest good, then they may hear it is time to let this relationship go, bless it for all the ways it has served them, seek to find peace with this person in their heart, and have faith knowing that a better situation is ahead. They can trust and make their peace with what is happening and move on.

"For most, this proposition seems painful, difficult, lonely, and scary. They think that the short-term solution of trying to convince their partner why they should stay is safer, happier, less scary, and less lonely. When you look at the two, you can see that in fact seeking peace and having faith is the only way to go, and yet in the moment, one would decide to convince the other over anything else or do whatever they can to avoid the pain. What they do not realize is how much pain they are already in at that moment. When one stops to acknowledge how much pain they are really in because of their fears, they would choose peace. Instead, what one has is the illusion that hope brings them in a short-term solution.

"In asking for that which is in your highest good, it is important to acknowledge that one does not know what is in their highest good. It is easy to think one knows, and yet the Truth of that is different indeed. You come to trust and understand what is in your highest good by putting things in God's Hands. It is easy to look at different options and think you know what is best, but to know what is truly in the highest good means that which may offer you the most learning, the most growth, the most evolution, the right opportunity to move in the direction that you are ultimately seeking or the one that will uncover for you something that you need. One cannot see into the future and know what would be best for them, and yet, in asking for that which is in your highest good, the universe will conspire to bring you toward it by knowing all things.

"You cannot make a mistake, and at the same time, there are opportunities, directions, and relationships that would give you everything if you are willing. Other opportunities will support you in the status quo and do not offer you that push to move in the direction that you are ultimately seeking. Oftentimes, you need a little shove to get there."

Prayer for Another

Candace: Holy Spirit, what about praying for another?

Holy Spirit: "Ultimately, every prayer is for the whole, for the Sonship, for God's Child. When you pray for yourself, you are ultimately praying for all. When you pray for another, you are ultimately praying for yourself. If you say a prayer for someone else, you are giving the gift of that prayer to all of God's Children because your instant of remembering God, venturing into Truth, and being in Reality is the gift that you give to the whole when you do it. Each moment that each perceived child of God experiences Truth is a moment that everyone can have that Truth.

"God does not answer worldly prayers in the way that you perceive. If you say a prayer asking for someone's health, God will not address the issue of this person's health. It will be up to that person and their mind to perceive their health differently. If it is that person's path to have a certain disease and struggle with that experience and learn and grow as a result of that, then they will continue to move along on that path. This is not conscious often times and one may be fighting their illness, but it is not something that you can change within their mind; only they can change that within their mind.

"When you say a prayer for someone's health, you can be aware that you are ultimately praying for your own health, and allow yourself to become more aware of how your thinking is impacting your health, perhaps in ways that you do not want. When you change your thinking about your health, you open the door for another to see that it is possible to change their thinking and that may be the biggest gift you can offer to the one you are praying for. And even if one sees that it is possible to affect their health with their thinking, they may still choose not to and that is their path.

"If you really want to pray for someone else, you can say, 'God, if it be in this person's highest good, would You help to reassure them that You are there with them always, that they are loved, that they are whole and safe in Your Arms?' Then you can know that this prayer will be answered because it is already done."

Prayer for Understanding

Candace: Holy Spirit, how do we pray when things aren't going as we would like?

Holy Spirit: "If your life is unfolding differently than you hoped or your life is devastating in some way, rather than pray for it to be different, rather than pray for how you think you want your life to be, it is important to pray for understanding. Herein lies the key to happiness.

"Pray for the peace that can come to you from understanding what is happening, why it is happening, and how it can ultimately serve you. It is so easy to mourn a loss, no matter what that is—a person, place, or a thing. It is so easy to fear a change. It is so easy to begrudge a difference and to blame God, when instead one could have faith that what is unfolding must be in their highest good and ask God for the understanding to go with that loss or change.

"In seeking understanding, you can experience your life in such a way that it is more of a free fall rather than a derailed train. It is the same life—the free fall or the derailed train—in one, there is faith and understanding, and in the other, there is blame and devastation. In praying for peace and understanding, you will always have that prayer answered."

Prayer in its Simplest Form

DavidPaul: Holy Spirit, what is the simplest form of prayer?

Holy Spirit: "Prayer is talking to God and that can take any form imaginable. The simplest, most truthful, and most profound prayer would be 'thank you.' 'Thank You, God, for everything You have given me,' while understanding that the majority of the gifts that God has given you have yet to be received in the sense of being understood or acknowledged. It is then easy to understand why prayer is even desired. It is not necessary because everything has already been given to you, but with the idea that you are separate from God, live in the world, struggle and suffer, and do without, prayer seems necessary indeed.

"If you are praying for what you know to be true, instead of asking for it, you can just give thanks for it. If you want to ask for what is in the highest good of two warring groups, for example, and you want to ask God to join them in their Right-Thinking, you can say, 'Thank You, God, for the ever presence of Truth within the minds of all of God's Children so that we may know what is best in every moment,' or something similar that acknowledges what is Real and True already.

"If you want to hear God, instead of saying, 'Please God, I want to hear your Voice in all that I do,' you can say instead, 'God, thank You for giving me your Voice that I may hear You in every moment that I choose. God, thank you for the opportunity of Right-Thinking in any moment.' In this way, you acknowledge and validate what really *is* rather than the thought of needing something, or wanting something, as if God would allow His Children to go out into the world without all of their needs met. It is not possible. Your needs have already all been met. Your prayer has been answered and the Holy Spirit has been given to you to choose, in any and every moment, that you may have peace and love and remembrance of the Truth of who you are.

"'Thank you, God, for the Peace and the Love and the Joy that I have.' You can say that prayer regardless of how you are feeling because, in Truth, you have been given Peace and Love and Joy and that is the Truth of who and what you are. It is only a thought that keeps you from It. The more that you acknowledge and validate the Truth, the more you will experience Truth in the world. 'Thank you, God, for putting the Holy Spirit into each perceived Child of God in the world so that I have the unending opportunity to hear your Voice in everyone I encounter. Thank you, God, for my true safety. Thank you that I need never fear because in Truth, I am always at Home with You.' When you have the thought of needing or wanting something that is Right-Minded, you can remember that you do have it. Give thanks for it, and you will start to bring it more into your awareness and experience and belief.

"God does not perceive the world because God only has full knowledge of Truth and there is no opposite to that. There are no lies. There are no illusions. There is no hate in opposition to God's Love or any other opposite you can think of. There is only Truth and the knowledge of that Truth; therefore, God cannot perceive the world or any of your needs in the world.

"God has given you the Holy Spirit to be able to perceive the illusion with you to then help you get to the other side. If the Holy Spirit were not willing to perceive the illusion, the Holy Spirit would not be able to help you out of it. When you have a situation in the world that is causing you pain or suffering, you can pray to the Holy Spirit to change your thinking about the situation. The Holy Spirit can then either remind you that this is all a dream or give you a perspective of Truth that allows you to have peace because you understand why what appears to be happening is happening. Your body, your family, your home, your job, where you live, and the rest of the world are all a dream.

"Eventually, your prayers can become very comfortable, fluid, loving, and warm. They can become an easy back and forth dialogue, back and forth in the sense of you giving thanks and feeling God's Presence, you giving acknowledgment and feeling God within your heart and mind, and you have a sense of your overall connectedness with God as a result. Prayer opens the door and God is waiting patiently on the other side of that door, at all times, in all situations, to join with you. Prayer is an experience, not a request. It is a joining, not a wanting. Prayer is an opening and a gift. Prayer is the gift itself rather than what it is you are praying for. Prayer is the answer to the prayer."

––––––––––

DavidPaul: How we came to write this book illustrates the power of using prayer in its simplest form. In 1999, I had the opportunity to work at America Online. Although I was excited to work at such a fast-growing Internet company and dreamed of making millions in stock options, I knew in my heart that I did not want a career in corporate America and that our life's work involved sharing the Voice of the Holy Spirit with others. Though that was true, we were not ready to pursue that dream with the Holy Spirit. We were just starting a family and thought we needed a good paying job to support ourselves in the high-priced Silicon Valley, so I took the job with one caveat—I would only commit to corporate life for four years...no matter what.

Before we knew it, the Internet bubble had burst, and three years later, our AOL stock options were worthless, literally not worth a dime. We were living month-to-month with little money in savings, and my job, with all of the downsizing and layoffs at AOL, was only becoming more difficult and stressful.

Around this time, we received guidance from the Holy Spirit to make a list of the most important things in our lives and to use that list to establish a family prayer. We were guided to write this prayer as if it were already true, as though we had already received all that we were asking for and wanting. We thought about our goals for quite awhile and then wrote the following prayer:

"Thank You, God, that we are a happy, healthy, three-parent family, living our soul purpose in union with the Holy Spirit, while being financially provided for in every way." (For us, the term three-parent family acknowledges that God is our daughter's true Parent, as well as ours.)

We were guided to say this prayer as often as possible throughout the day. Even though it was difficult at times to force this reality upon our minds when we were not feeling happy or healthy or financially provided for, saying the prayer in this way helped us to literally form this reality within our minds.

Practically to the day of my four year anniversary at AOL, with my stock options fully vested and still worthless, my hands started hurting. With each passing day, they became worse and worse. Soon, I could no longer type, and it was becoming very difficult to do my job. Before I knew it, my career at AOL started going down the drain. In our quest to find a cure for my hands, we did a lot of soul searching and checked in with the Holy Spirit regularly. Eventually, we came to view my disability as an opportunity to change the course of our lives.

Around this time, Candace and our daughter went to visit Candace's father who was living on eleven acres in Oregon. While Candace was there, she fell in love with being on the land, watching our daughter freely come and go from her father's rural house.

Back at AOL, the fear, control, and uncertainty within the company was at an all-time high. Management was talking out loud of impending layoffs, and it had been rumored that my position was among them. After checking in with the Holy

Spirit, we decided to put our townhouse on the market so we wouldn't be burdened with a house payment if I lost my job. The next day, our next door neighbors, who were renting their unit, said they were interested in buying our townhouse, which meant no realtor fees or open houses. We jumped at the chance.

We immediately called Candace's father and asked if we could live in the guest house on his property. Because his tenants had unexpectedly vacated only weeks before, he excitedly said yes. One week later, I was laid off from work. Three weeks later, escrow closed on our townhouse, and that day we moved to Oregon. If we liquidated all of our assets and lived simply, we would have enough money to last us possibly two years, which would be enough time to follow our dream of writing this book with the Holy Spirit.

One month after selling our townhouse and moving to Oregon, we found a wonderful preschool for our daughter three mornings a week, and with no corporate job keeping us busy, we began writing this book with the Holy Spirit. In so doing, we are truly fulfilling our dream of being a three-parent family, living our soul purpose in union with the Holy Spirit, while being financially provided for in every way. And we have God and the Holy Spirit to thank for guiding and supporting us every step of the way.

Exercise—Joining in Prayer

Holy Spirit: "Set aside a certain time each day for prayer. This need only be a few minutes or it can be as long as you like, but have a certain time every day that you set aside to connect with God. This might be the first thing you do in the morning, the last thing you do at night, something you do every day during your lunch break, or at any other time during the day. Regardless, do try to give yourself a consistent moment that you reserve for this connection.

"If you decide to use the first minutes of your waking for prayer, then as you begin to come out of your sleep, remind yourself that this is your prayer time and begin to prepare yourself for that. You might continue lying down. You may decide to sit up. You may have your eyes open or closed, be in a particular position, or have your hands and legs in a certain position. It only matters what is comfortable or meaningful for you. It is oftentimes helpful to have some sort of ritual, meaning that you use the same sort of process or behavior each time.

"In addition, remind yourself that prayer is not asking God for something, but rather the opportunity to connect with God, to open the door to God. The door is always there and from God's side, it is always open, so the intent to pray in this way allows the door on your side to become unlocked.

"Begin to focus on God. You might say, 'Hello,' or 'Good morning, God, it's me,' or begin whatever type of dialogue you would like. You may want to give thanks for your rest and the new day. You may want to share something that is in your heart and mind to share. You may want to ask a question, or you may want to complain about a situation. Regardless, do so with the intent, first and foremost, to connect with God, to connect with a good Friend, to connect with this loving Parent or Companion.

"You can then rest from your communication and imagine, if you like, hearing what God has to say back to you. The Holy Spirit will deliver the Messages directly to you, swiftly and with love, if you listen. You may experience a sense of peace or gratitude or some insight or awareness about a situation. You may perceive something differently. It does not matter, just that you use this time with the intent to connect, to join, and to share with God.

"Give thanks for your joining, and when you are complete, go about your day while doing the best you can to be mindful of the experience you have just had. You may want to consider beginning and ending your day in this way. Of course, you are welcome to join with God as often as possible, as often as you like or would enjoy, or as often as it occurs to you.... God is always waiting patiently for you to unlock that door."

Chapter Highlights

"Prayer is the opportunity to transcend the world in any given moment and connect with what is really True and Real."

"If you want worldly things such as a family, a home, a job, good health, or whatever it may be, you can ask God to join you in your thinking to be able to manifest what is best for you."

"In praying for the highest good in any situation, you can trust that whatever is truly the best for one's path will unfold."

"When you pray for yourself, you are ultimately praying for all. When you pray for another, you are ultimately praying for yourself."

"In seeking understanding, you can experience your life in such a way that it is more of a free fall rather than a derailed train. It is the same life—the free fall or the derailed train—in one, there is faith and understanding, and in the other, there is blame and devastation. In praying for peace and understanding, you will always have that prayer answered."

"Prayer is talking to God and that can take any form imaginable. The simplest, most truthful, and most profound prayer would be 'thank you.'"

10

Meditation

"When one quiets the mind,
they create an invitation to God
to join with them."

Holy Spirit: "It can be difficult to hear God's Voice over the noise of the world because the noise and the world are outside of you. There is a place you can go where the world does not exist, and that is within. When you go within, you leave the world and you step into a quiet place where God can enter. God does not enter the world, so God's pathway to you is through Right-Mindedness and the Holy Spirit. By going within, quieting the mind, and inviting God to join you in this place of Truth, you cannot help but hear God's Voice. It is all that is left in the quietness."

Setting the Stage

DavidPaul: Holy Spirit, how does meditation relate to hearing God's Voice?

Holy Spirit: "It is through meditation that one sets the stage for listening to God. Part of that preparation involves making a date with God, just as you would with anyone you wanted to engage in relationship with. If one really wanted to become married and have a family, for example, they would likely have as their priority clearing their calendar, meeting people, setting up dates, making reservations, getting tickets, dressing up, brushing their teeth, going on dates and everything else they need to do to truly connect with someone. They do this over and over and over again until eventually they make a connection with someone who wants to have a life with them. It is the same in your relationship with God. If you want to have a lifelong partnership with God, then you court God. You set up the date, the time, the place, the reservations, the tickets, etc., whatever that looks like metaphorically, so that you can honor that time and give it the value that it truly has. You would approach meditation in the same way. It is a very revered time that one would establish with God on a regular basis.

"Meditation dims the chatter of the world and the voice of the ego so that you can more easily join with God and hear the Voice of Truth within you. You do this physically by first finding a quiet place or room to sit and be still, turning off the ringers on your phones, putting a *Do Not Disturb* sign on your door, or whatever you need to do to literally close yourself off from the world so that you can have your date with God.

"Generally speaking, it is important to sit upright rather than lie down in meditation. For nearly every one, if you lie down and meditate, you will fall asleep and then that is called a nap, not meditation. If you are so tired that sitting there is impossible, you can either get up and move around and attempt to re-energize yourself and then sit back down, or you can lie down and rest for little bit and then sit back up and try again. If you need to rest, try to give yourself enough time to meditate after your rest so that it doesn't turn into just a nap. You may find that after some rest it becomes very simple to focus in this way.

"One may also find a particular sitting position to be more comfortable than another. In general, it's good to sit in a chair and to have your feet on the floor to help you be more awake and present. If you are comfortable sitting on the floor or on a cushion with your legs crossed lotus style, of course, that is fine as well. For some, there is effort in sitting this way and in holding their back up. They often become more focused on that than on allowing their mind to become emptied and open for a connection with God. There are no rules; just find a position that truly serves you.

"If you have a situation that is weighing heavily on your mind or distracting you in your meditation and you cannot overcome it, you can ask the Holy Spirit to be with you and to help restore you to Right-Thinking in that particular situation so that you can have your peace and your connectedness with God. You can ask the Holy Spirit for a perspective on that situation that allows you to understand your part in it, or to accept what you think you may have done, or to accept or understand what you think another may have done. Eventually you may come to understand that none of those things actually happened. It was only the way your mind perceived them and now your mind is free again to connect with God.

These encounters and situations are fabricated by the ego as very efficient and effective distractions from God. Once you have peace with something, your mind is then free to connect with Truth once again."

Creating a Practice

Holy Spirit: "It seems simple to say that prayer is talking to God and meditation is listening to God, but that is the truth. If you want to connect with God, you can begin the conversation with prayer and you can listen to the response that God or the Holy Spirit has for you through the practice of meditation because God's Voice exists in the quietness of your Right-Mind. To attain this connection or engage in this conversation, you have to go to where the other party is, and that is not in the world—it is not in the loudness and the chaos of the world—but in the quietness of your Right-Mind. To go there requires a practice, and that practice would be any form of meditation that can restore you to your Right-Mind so that you can go where God is, where God's Voice is, and join Him there. God's Voice is the stepping stone to God.

"Certainly, you are One with God and that has never changed. Yet from your perspective that the world is real and that you are separate, going through the Holy Spirit is the most efficient way, and the practice of meditation is what can take you there. Of course, one can become very desperate, pleading, begging, despondent, on their knees, and they may seek and find God in that moment and that may serve them in that moment and that is great, but they do not want to have to be desperate and pleading and on their knees every day to connect with God. It would be so much nicer to just sit quietly in a room with the door closed and attempt to focus inward and get to that place of Right-Mindedness so that you can have this ongoing relationship through this ongoing practice that can be effortless and nurturing and fulfilling beyond your wildest dreams, and you can spare your knees at the same time.

"Whenever you have a thought that causes you pain, makes you sad, frustrated, angry, disappointed, depressed, or longing, you can seek Right-Mindedness in whatever way might be right for you. You can ask, 'Is that thought true?' or you may take a break, sit down, breathe, and ask to be restored to Right-Mindedness. You may ask the Holy Spirit to be with you and help you to overcome those thoughts so that you can see the Truth of the situation. The more that you have a meditation practice in your life, the easier it will be for you to return to that practice in your times of need. It is through that practice that you will connect with the only thing that can really help you, and that is the most wonderful gift you can give yourself and all of God's Children."

Exercises—Quieting the Mind

DavidPaul: The purpose of meditation is to focus your mind in such a way that you no longer hear the voice of the ego and can instead join with God, God's Voice, Truth, Source, Peace, Joy, or whatever it is you are seeking. Before reading the following exercises, it's important to acknowledge and validate what you are already doing to quiet your mind.

If you don't have a meditation practice, take some time to think about what methods or practices have worked for you in the past. Chances are you have done something that has allowed you to be connected with Source. You may have read a specific book, taken a vacation by yourself, said a particular prayer or mantra, hiked to a beautiful place, or done any number of things that assisted you in feeling connected.

The exercises below are an option for those who do not have a regular meditation practice or for those who are looking to explore other methods. They are not intended to be all encompassing or definitive. If you presently have a practice that helps you to quiet your mind, by all means continue to use it. The possibilities for quieting the mind are truly unlimited.

Visualization

Many people enjoy using visualization to connect with God. Visualization can help to focus the mind on Truth. Any visualization that serves this purpose may be used. Below are a few examples.

Bulldozing the Mind

With your eyes closed, imagine your mind as a lush and beautiful garden that has not been tended to in some time. The flowers may have shriveled up. The delicious fruit might have fallen to the ground and become rotten. The soil may have dried up or weeds may have taken over.

Now imagine that there is a large bulldozer in front of you. Use this bulldozer to break up the dry and hardened soil. Use it to turn the rocky earth. As you do, the rich soil that has always been there soon rises to the surface. Continue to turn the soil over and over until you see that the earth has become soft, moist, and fertile once again. This may take a little time.

When the soil is ready, ask God for new seeds to plant. Place them in the rich and fertile soil and then water them. Tend them and give them plenty of sunshine. Eventually, new life begins to sprout and grow. Before long, your garden is lush and beautiful once again.

Note: This visualization may take you thirty minutes or it may take you two months. In either case, visualizing a barren garden does not make it true nor does it mean that you will not hear the Holy Spirit until your garden is bursting with life. It is only to say that you can visualize breaking up the parts of your mind that are not fully receptive to hearing God's Voice. With this intention, this visualization may begin to open your mind to receiving God's Voice in new or different ways.

A Bridge to the Mind of God

Holy Spirit: "Since the Holy Spirit is the Bridge to the Mind of God, close your eyes and envision that you are standing on one side of a bridge and God's Mind is on the other side of the bridge. This bridge can look any way you like. It might cross over water. It could be a heavenly structure extending from one cloud to another with nothing below it. It may be an image of a rainbow—whatever comes to you as you close your eyes and go within.

"Imagine yourself walking up to that bridge, making a decision to cross it, and then moving across that bridge until you are half way across it. This is where you can release any thoughts of the ego from your mind to be cleansed and transformed into Right-Minded thoughts. You may release judgment, sadness, envy, guilt, anger, or any other emotions you no longer want. They will all be washed away and transformed.

"When you are ready, continue crossing the bridge until you reach the other side. This is the Mind of God. This is where all are One. You have now entered into a sacred place within yourself where you can access all Truths. It is familiar territory to you. Setting an intention to go here when you want to communicate with God's Voice will bring clarity to the experience."

Your Meeting Place with God

Holy Spirit: "Imagine a meeting place where you and God join together to connect and communicate. This is a place where you can step out of the world and rendezvous with God, a place where you know God is waiting for you. It can be as beautiful, as simple, and as sweet or mundane a place as you desire. Knowing that God is joining you there, chances are it will be special.

"It might be a place that you dream of being. It may be surrounded by mountains, or water, or something that allows it to be a place that is only entered by you, God, and God's Voice. Over time, having a consistent image related to joining with God can make it easier and easier to get there, to be there, and to join with God in this way. This is not a place that is outside of you. It is a place that is within you where God is always waiting to join with you."

Golden Light

With your eyes closed, visualize someone standing in front of you. This could be someone you know or don't know, someone you care about, or someone you have an issue with. As you gaze upon them, you see a golden light beginning to spin around them like a long piece of yarn. The light slowly continues to circle around their body, and as it does, it begins to form a ball of golden light around them. The light continues around and around until it eventually becomes completely solid.

When there are no holes or gaps in the ball of light and it is completely surrounding the person in front of you, imagine that the ball of light begins to radiate infinitely inward toward their body, filling every cell of their body along the way. When this inward journey is complete, imagine that the ball of light begins to radiate outward, beyond the boundaries of the universe and into infinity. Soon, all that exists is golden light and a thin outline of the person standing in front of you.

This vision is symbolic of the Truth of who they are. As you gaze upon their essence, speak these or other words of Truth to them, "I give you the Peace of Christ. Accept it, for this is who you are, and you are blessed above all things."

Breathing

Holy Spirit: "For some, breathing is a technique that can help the mind become focused on one thing. Listening to our breath and focusing on our breath can help us slow down and go within.

"There are a variety of methods one can use. You may sit down and begin to take deep breaths in and out, in and out, focusing on your breath exclusively. While you are doing that, you may also use some sort of mantra. For example, you may hold one thought as you breathe in and another as you breathe out. You may breathe in and say silently to yourself, 'I am,' and you may breathe out saying silently to yourself, 'at peace,' or 'loved,' or 'connected with God,' or any statement that feels right to you.

"You may want to breathe in through your nose and out through your mouth, or vice versa; or you may prefer breathing in and out through only your nose. You might want to use a form of yogic breath work where your mouth is closed and yet you hear your breathing within your esophagus. Or, you might breathe in for a certain count—1, 2, 3, 4, then hold your breath 1, 2, 3, 4, then breathe out 1, 2, 3, 4—so that all of the counts are the same, continuing to do this until there is a natural rhythm.

"It does not matter which technique you follow. Do what is easy and natural for you so that you can focus inwardly rather than thinking about your day, the dishes, your mate, what food you are going to make for a party on Saturday, and so on. Focusing on your breath simply allows you to focus on the here and now. Breathe in whatever way allows you to be comfortable, to become more relaxed, to get into a meditative state, and allow this focus on the breath to keep you from the distractions of the mind. As you focus on your breath, you can oftentimes be transported to a meditative state where you are seemingly beyond the world. You may find after just breathing consciously for a period of time that the world has fallen away and that you have become very still and quiet within."

Silence

Holy Spirit: "You may have periods of time that you set aside to *not* communicate. You may have hours or days of silence. You may set aside one period of time each week where you do not communicate out loud. This is a quiet and reflective time. You can let those around you know that you will not be communicating during that time. Let the phone and the door go unanswered and listen instead to Who is calling you within.

"If you are having periods of time in your life that are silent times, as they become more reflective, as they become more quiet, the mind begins to quiet. Your whole inside begins to quiet, and this creates the opportunity to hear that which has always been there, God's Voice. The Holy Spirit cannot shout over all the noise of the world, but rather waits for a quiet opening to make Its Presence known."

Sound and Mantras

Holy Spirit: "You may close your eyes and not focus on your breathing but focus instead on a particular sound. In some cultures, it would be the sound of *Om* or *Huu* or something like this. Saying it aloud or in your mind helps to quiet the mind, leaving it open for communion with God.

"If you don't have a specific sound in mind, you might have a statement, mantra, invitation, or prayer that you say over and over again—'I am one with God,' or 'I am at peace,' or 'everything is perfect,' or 'I am as God created me,' whatever statement or thought you have that serves you. Repeat that thought over and over again in your mind as a way of allowing that thought to become true for you in your thinking. Saying something over and over again or listening to something repeatedly in meditation or throughout your day helps your mind stay focused on thoughts that serve you.

"You may prefer to practice this while taking a walk. (This would not include walking with someone else or in a group.) As you walk, you might hold one thought with one step and a different thought with the next—with your first step, 'I am,' and with your next step, 'with God,' and so on as you walk; or you may say a prayer over and over again as you walk. How you meditate while walking is irrelevant if, in fact, it serves you in your goal of connecting with or hearing God's Voice."

Feeling

Holy Spirit: "One way to connect with God is to simply sit and feel His Presence, feel His Love, feel His Grace surrounding you, within you. You may envision yourself in God's Arms or with God wrapped around you like a blanket. You might be sitting in the palm of God's Hand, safe and secure. Use whatever visualization allows you to experience being cared for or loved or watched over by God, and then allow yourself to feel what that feels like to just feel God's Love, God's Presence. You can feel it in you, around you, through you—focus on that feeling;

wallow in that feeling. Allow yourself to go as deep into that feeling as you can. You may laugh. You may cry. You may scream. You may be very, very quiet and still. You may be all of these things in the process of feeling God.

"God is ever ready to join with you, and as you set your intention and focus on connecting in this way, you cannot help but experience this joining. When you allow yourself to feel how it feels so that you are completely filled and over-flowing with the feeling of God and you think you might burst, you give yourself an inkling of what your true relationship with God really is."

Chapter Highlights

"It is through meditation that one sets the stage for listening to God. Part of that preparation involves making a date with God, just as you would with anyone you wanted to engage in relationship with."

––––––––––

"It seems simple to say that prayer is talking to God and meditation is listening to God, but that is the truth."

––––––––––

"The purpose of meditation is to focus your mind in such a way that you no longer hear the voice of the ego and can instead join with God, God's Voice, Truth, Source, Peace, Joy, or whatever it is you are seeking."

11

Hearing God's Voice

"Every time you hear a loving thought
or speak a loving word,
you are hearing God's Voice."

Holy Spirit: "Hearing God's Voice is everything you have longed for, everything you have dreamed of, and what you have been convinced is impossible. Hearing God's Voice nourishes you in a way that you could never be nourished in the world. Hearing this Voice is an experience that cannot be contained within the body because, of course, the body is not real. It is bigger than you perceive yourself and more impacting. It is different than you imagine because it is not of this world. When you hear this Voice, you are transcending the world in that moment. This Voice restores you to all that is True and Real and also guides and directs you in what is not real so that you can notice the difference and eventually leave the world behind."

DavidPaul's Story Continued

DavidPaul: Listening to the White Brotherhood growing up, experiencing the Truth of who I am while reading a channeled transcript from Jesus, and literally being brought back to life in Hawaii by the Voice of the Holy Spirit, it's easy to see why I would be so motivated to hear God's Voice. As a result of these experiences, a deep desire to have and use this resource for myself began to grow within me.

I first felt it in Hawaii. It deepened throughout my travels around the world, and it blossomed into an irresistible passion upon my return to the mainland. I practiced and practiced, tried and tried, and surrendered with all my might to hear this Voice within me, but no matter what I did, I just couldn't hear It. I'd meditate for hours, reach a place of complete silence and peace within me, surrender and listen in every way I could imagine, but no matter how hard I tried or didn't try, it was always the same—I'd eventually give up in frustration, disappointment, and sometimes anger.

Unconsciously surrounding myself with even more motivation to hear this Voice, I, of course, had five other friends who could also hear a clear and distinct voice within them. One channeled Gaia. Another channeled Elijah. Another channeled God knows who…. The point is, they all had a voice within them that they could use to hear truth and guidance in their lives. It may not have been the Voice of the Holy Spirit, but it was a voice nonetheless. Why could they do it and not me?

Over the course of several years, I probably prayed to hear the Holy Spirit at least a thousand times. I asked my friends how they did it, and I asked the spirits they talked to how to do it as well. I did everything they told me to do—every exercise, every meditation, every prayer, but nothing seemed to help. My passion, commitment, and drive to hear and open to the Holy Spirit would grow with every exercise I was given, but I would quickly tumble into depression, anger, and hopelessness after weeks or months of trying with no success. This was so frustrating and devastating that I would sometimes cry in defeat. Eventually, after several years of struggle, I finally gave up. While a part of me felt like a failure, another part of me felt relieved to give up the fight. I made a commitment to stop trying to hear God's Voice within me, and it felt good.

A couple of years later, when Candace and I eventually became a couple and started checking in with the Holy Spirit on a regular basis, my desire and passion to hear this Voice was rekindled and I began to ask the Holy Spirit for guidance on how to open up to hearing this Voice within me. As a result, the Holy Spirit suggested that I begin by asking God for signs.

So before getting out of bed each morning, I would ask God for communication about something that was going on in my life. I would then hold the intention to receive His answer in some way throughout the day. If I didn't know the answer before climbing back into bed that evening, I would ask the same question the following morning. At first, it would take me three or four days to receive the answer. Over time, it became easier and easier to notice the signs.

Eventually, I was recognizing the signs on a daily basis and was truly enjoying the process. (See page 125 for communication about signs.)

After several months of receiving signs, the Holy Spirit suggested that I begin to hear God's Voice through conversation with other people. So I began to hold the intention that whoever I spoke with throughout the day would share God's Words with me. I practiced this exercise for several months. It was tricky at first, but as I continued to practice, I began to hear God's Voice through all kinds of people, even my boss. Sometimes, the words were literal. Other times, I would hear God's Messages to me as if they were superimposed over the Words that were actually being said.

Eventually, I came to see that it was all about perception, and as time went on, I started feeling very fulfilled in my communication with God. I may not have been hearing a distinct and audible voice within me, but I was hearing God's Voice nonetheless, and it felt good.

One spring morning in March of 2000, Candace was about to head off for a two-week retreat to do "The Work" with Byron Katie. While we were lying in bed that morning, we read from *A Course in Miracles*. The lesson of the day was, "God's Voice speaks to me all through the day." As Candace read the lesson out loud, I got really upset. I interpreted the lesson to mean hearing a specific Voice within me. I was so tired of getting my hopes up and not having it happen that I just started fuming! I could barely contain my anger.

Candace wasn't aware of what was going on for me, so she finished reading the lesson, closed her eyes, and began to check in with the Holy Spirit. As the Holy Spirit spoke, my anger began to dissipate. At one point, a huge wave of peace came over me and the Holy Spirit said something through Candace that It had never said before.... The Holy Spirit told me to open my mouth and allow the Voice to come through me.

Although I was scared, I opened my mouth and started to speak. To my surprise, out came the Holy Spirit! I don't remember how long I spoke or even what I said, but it was one of the happiest moments of my life. Tears fell from Candace's eyes as the Words came through me. It was truly a heavenly moment.

To our surprise, we discovered a few weeks later that our daughter, Hannah, was conceived that very morning. I've been hearing this Voice within me ever since....

Prerequisites

DavidPaul: Holy Spirit, what are the prerequisites to hearing God's Voice?

Holy Spirit: "All that one needs in order to hear God's Voice is the desire. If the desire is there, the Voice will be given. That is God's Law. If you desire to hear God's Voice, then you will and that is the beginning and the end of that. How you get there is another matter. How you get to the place of having desire is each one's fate. The desire is there for everyone. It is just a matter of remembering it.

"For some, the desire is so strong that nothing else is sought over a lifetime. For others, it is forgotten completely, and yet it is the same desire within each one. If you seek to hear God, you will—in all ways, in all things, through all means—and it is up to you to receive the Messages. If you desire to hear God, all around you is God speaking, but if you do not like the delivery or you do not value the delivery, it cannot be received. If you are open and willing to allow God's Voice to take any form through your trust and your faith, by desiring to hear God, you will. You can hear God in everything—in the silence, in the chaos, in conversations over the phone, in a book.

"It is important to not be attached to a certain delivery but rather be open to all things. If you desire to hear God's Voice within your heart and mind, then hold a very clear intention for that, a very clear plan for that to unfold in your life, and be clear that you are willing to make whatever seeming sacrifices are needed. This is said tongue-in-cheek because the sacrifices one makes to hear God's Voice are so meaningless and yet can seem like everything. You may lose that which you think you value. You may lose that which you think is important to you. You may lose that which you think matters to you in the process of hearing God's Voice because you have been convinced by the ego that everything you see is real, that everything you have matters, and that everything you want is important. Once you hear God's Voice, the ego falls away in that instant. You can only hear one or the other. It is not possible for them to speak over each other.

"As you open to hearing God's Voice, the ego will become quiet for that moment and all that you think matters will fall away; all that you value will become meaningless and that which is True will rest in your heart and your mind—Heaven. In that moment, you will be in Heaven and the world will be gone.

"You must be willing to give up all that you seem to be attached to now in order to hear Truth, because Truth does not involve anything in the world. Hearing Truth can feel like a very humbling experience because you are so used to being right, being the best, or being first. In the presence of Truth, none of that exists. You have to be willing to no longer be the best at this or first at that or have your identity be associated with something in the world. The Truth is that you are a Child of God, complete and whole and loved just as you are, just because you are, which has nothing to do with what you do in the world, how you do it, who you do it with, or anything else.

"For some, the risk of giving up all that is familiar, known, comfortable, rewarding, validating, and esteeming is too high a price to pay to hear God's Voice, and yet you cannot forget that what you desire is to know the Truth. There is so much to hearing God; it goes on forever because, in Truth, that is all there is."

Exercises—Hearing God's Voice

DavidPaul: There are countless ways to hear God's Voice. In the course of uncovering this Voice within ourselves, Candace and I have both used a wide variety of methods to strengthen our openness and ability to hear God's Voice with confidence and faith. Some of these methods are listed below along with step-by-step instructions and communication from the Holy Spirit. These exercises are not intended to be exhaustive, but they may provide a starting point for strengthening your faith, openness, and ability to hear God's Voice—'in whatever way that happens for you. While the exercises are specific, feel free to adapt them as necessary to meet your style, personality, or needs in any given moment.

Holy Spirit: "Everything can be used as a tool or means to hear God. You give everything the meaning that it has, so you can allow anything and everything to serve as your communication with God. It is all a matter of perspective.

"There are people who train themselves that when the phone rings, they think, 'Oh, that's God calling.' They pick it up and they experience God on the other end. Regardless of the situation, what it's about, or whoever may be calling, they experience that God is on the other end and take from that communication whatever Message God has for them.

"You can allow everything to serve you in hearing God's Voice and allow everything you see and hear and do to be of God, strictly from how you approach it within your mind. You can use anything as a means to hear God, and for some, it can be helpful to use a consistent method."

Spiritual Books

Holy Spirit: "Reading a book that is filled with Truth, you can gain more of a sense of Who and What God really is and as such be able to experience a deeper sense of connectedness and communion so that there is some type of communication happening back and forth, whether that is obvious or not.

"There is also the experience of just taking a book off the shelf and opening it to any page with the intention that whatever Message God has for you, whatever direction or insight you need next, it will be there on that page. It may mean something different to someone else, but as you read it, you will glean your own message from it."

Steps

1. Determine what you want to know, understand, or receive and then share that with God in whatever ways you wish.

2. Pray or hold the intention that you are being guided to the right book, the right page, and the right paragraph to receive the answer or reply that is in your highest good.

3. You may already have a book in mind or not. If you do not and you are selecting a book from a bookshelf, allow yourself to reach for a book naturally, having faith that whatever book you select is perfect.

4. Open the book and point to a paragraph.

5. Read what you have pointed to and allow the words or the message to sink in. They may or may not be obvious. If you do not understand, continue to seek its meaning. As you hold the intention to hear the Truth that it has for you, you will open to hearing the Message that God has given you.

Spiritual Cards or Runes

Holy Spirit: "One can use various types of spiritual cards, tarot cards, or runes with intention so that when you hold a thought, say a prayer, seek an answer, or seek guidance or connection, you will again be able to receive communication from God as you turn over a card or pick up a stone, and with that intention, you can trust the communication."

Steps

1. Determine what you want to know, understand, or receive and then share that with God in whatever ways you wish.

2. Pray or hold the intention that you are being guided to the right card, the right stone, or the right symbol, whatever that may be, that is in your highest good.

3. Select and turn over the card or stone without analyzing or second-guessing your natural impulse.

4. Read the message(s) provided in the book that came with the cards or runes or be aware of any thoughts or insights that come to your mind. If you do not understand the answer that comes to you, continue to seek its meaning. As you hold the intention to hear the Truth that it has for you, you will continue to open to receiving the Message that God has given you.

Signs

Holy Spirit: "You may have a particular situation going on that is very troubling or confusing, and you are in need of clear direction. As you go through your day, you can ask for signs. When you have the intention that God will give you signs and show you the way, you will be able to see the signs. They are always there, and yet without the intention to see them, you miss them. You have gotten to this point using signs, whether they have been consciously witnessed or not.

"You can determine for yourself that whatever messages and directions you need will be given to you. Then as you go through your day, you might literally see a sign with guidance on it. You might open a newspaper and see what it is that you need to do. You may get a phone call, encounter a person, experience a situation, or witness something that you realize is the answer for you. It is powerful to do this in troubling times and yet you can go through your whole life every day asking for signs, receiving signs, and allowing their messages to be made clear to you so that you move continually in the direction of Truth. When you are very clear about what you desire, you will be given all that you need to get there."

Steps

1. Become clear about what you are seeking and then ask God to show you a sign as His reply to your request or question.

2. Allow yourself to be completely open as to what the sign may look like and how it may be given.

3. Pray or hold the intention that you will recognize the sign as it is given.

4. Be mindful and aware throughout your day or week of what you see, think, hear, or experience, knowing that God's communication to you may take any form.

5. Be patient and have faith that you and God are working together to create a sign that you will receive.

Dreams

Holy Spirit: "Just as you imagine that you are living a life in the world in the body, that your body tires and you rest, you sleep and you dream, that is what is representative of your 'real life'—you are in a very long sleep with long vivid dreams. Just as you glean messages from the lives you appear to live and the experiences you appear to have, you are really just having a dream. And when you have a dream within the dream—when you are in the body and you rest and you sleep and you have a dream—you can glean messages from these dreams as well.

"You may wake up in the night or in the morning with a dream on your mind and you might ask within you for insight or direction as to what that dream means and allow yourself to receive whatever answer or message you are given. When one doesn't ask, the answer does not come. So in asking, your answer will come. It is only a matter of when. Allow your dreams to serve you if you desire, just as what appears to be your life now is serving you."

Steps

1. Ask the Holy Spirit to help you understand what message your dream has for you and then listen for the Holy Spirit's reply.

2. Be aware of any thoughts, feelings, or insights that come to you and trust what you receive.

3. If you do not experience receiving the answer right then, allow yourself to receive the answer later in the day or in the week.

4. Be open to receiving the answer in any form, as a sign, an insight, through something you read or hear, etc.

Note: You can also seek guidance and direction from the Holy Spirit before going to bed and hold the intention to receive the answer while you sleep or in your dreams.

Listening to Others

Holy Spirit: "In remembering that God's Voice speaks through all of God's Children, you can allow yourself to trust and have faith that God can speak to you through another. So, you have stated your prayer, your intention, your desire for Truth, and then someone in front of you in the grocery line turns around and makes a statement to you or a cashier or another person in line and it is exactly what you need to hear to remind you of Truth. You can do this for direct guidance, for remembrance, for an answer, or whatever you need. Just hold the intention that whoever stands near you will share God's Words with you and you will be able to pick out the message as it is being delivered.

"It may be that you are out in the world and you hear a child say, 'Let's play!' and it just rings true for you. There is something about that tiny communication and you say, 'Oh, I need to play. I need to have more play,' and you bring yourself to a park, or you play a game, or you do something more playfully rather than seriously in your life. You approach things with a more playful attitude.

"It can be the simplest, most mundane, everyday type of communication, but with the intention that you will hear God in what another speaks, you will hear a message and there will be a certain feeling or experience within you that you know this message was meant for you. It rings true for you and you can take it and apply it in your life in ways that truly serve you."

Steps

1. Pray or hold the intention that whoever you are with is sharing God's Words with you.

2.   Each time you hear someone speak, remind yourself that you are listening to God's Voice.

3.   Ask yourself, "What is God saying to me through this person?" The message may be literal, symbolic, implied, or a variety of other things. It may come through the person's words, their emotion, tone, or intention. It does not matter. If the answer or message is not apparent, ask again, "What is God saying to me through this person?

4.   Trust the thoughts, insights, and messages that come to you.

Speaking Truth

Holy Spirit: "You can also have the intention of being a messenger to another. You can have the intention that whatever it is that another needs to hear, you are able to say. You can ask that it come through you in your communications with another and state that intention each day or before certain encounters so that you will know that whatever it is you are saying is the appropriate thing for that situation and you can trust that it is right.

"The goal is not to have the person hear God, because that is their business, their choice, their path, and their free will. Your intention is that you speak messages of Truth, and that is different. What they do with that, if anything, is up to them. For you, you gain the validation or acknowledgment for having had the thought to do that, the intention to follow through, and the willingness to allow the message of Truth to come through you, and that's the end of it. Enjoy it for the experience that it is rather than what someone else may gain from it."

Steps

1.   Say a prayer or hold the intention that you can and will speak God's Words in a given situation or throughout your day, to a specific person, or to anyone around you.

2.   Continue to hold this intention as you speak.

3.   Knowing that God speaks to people wherever they are and in whatever ways they are able to receive, allow your words to flow freely. Trust what you say and how you say it.

4.   When you are finished speaking, thank God for the opportunity to share His Words and give thanks to yourself for being willing to share Them.

Journaling

Holy Spirit: "For many people, the opportunity to sit with themselves, God, a notebook, and a pen is something that is very intimate and very rewarding. One can sit with a pen and paper and have the intention that God communicate with them, to them, or through them, and then begin to write down the thoughts they have while they are intending to be connected with God. It doesn't mean necessarily that a big booming Voice speaks in their head and tells them all of the secrets of the universe. It means that you may have certain thoughts come to mind. You may have insights, perspectives, or situations come up and you can make note of those and put them into a journal.

"Regardless of whether you understand or receive great value from these thoughts in the moment, you can later sit with this journal and look at what is written there. If you do this on an ongoing basis, you will begin to see themes and messages that carry over repeatedly. These are things you would want to take notice of.

"A situation may continue to come to mind, and as you make note of it, you might become aware that it is something that is unresolved and needs to be completed. You may notice that there are some things you need to do something about. You might become aware that these things are either distractions away from God or things that will take you closer in your communion with God. Writing these things down can help you have a sense of these within your mind. It is an exercise in being aware of your thoughts, and as you continue to intend to be in communion with God and hear God, you can use the thoughts that come up to help you deepen your relationship with God.

"You may have thoughts that this isn't real or possible, such as 'I can't communicate with God.' Make note of that and ask yourself, 'Is it true? Is it true that I can't communicate with God in this way?' Absolutely not. Give yourself the freedom of recognizing that those thoughts are just universal thoughts that the ego promotes. There are many people who believe that it is not possible to communicate with God, and that doesn't have to be your truth. In your reality, it is possible. Therefore, you will be able to.

"As you become aware of what goes on in your mind, you can work with your thinking. You can become aware of what you need to shift or change perspective on so that you can see things differently. You can gain messages of Truth that can carry you through the day or bring peace to a situation. You can become aware of how to handle something or know that something needs to be taken care of. This then becomes prayer and meditation with God that you are simply taking notes on."

Steps

1. Sit alone in a quiet place where there are no distractions.

2. Say a prayer or hold the intention that God is communicating with you, to you, and through you.

3. As you continue to hold this intention, write down any thoughts that come to you. Don't worry if they are only single words, repeating words, or sentence fragments. You may acknowledge a particular thought or you may just have an impulse to write something down. Allow yourself to write freely without judgment or analysis.

4. When you are finished, thank God for working with you to hear and manifest His Voice.

5. Periodically review your journal for themes and messages.

Hearing God's Voice Within You

Holy Spirit: "When one prays, they are communicating with God. They are the one doing the talking. When one meditates, they are listening to God and God is the One doing the talking. The most beneficial tool for being able to have an ongoing communication with God comes from meditation, which can include prayer.

"If you are able to maintain your focus, attention, and intention on God, it is difficult for other things to distract you away. When your focus is only on clearing your mind, being quiet, or emptying in some way, there is more of an opportunity for everything to come in and fill the mind. When you have your mind stayed on God and you continue to reconnect with that thought and that intention over and over again, when you are just there to join with, experience, and hear God, when you are very willing and able to listen to whatever it is God has to say to you or share with you, there is no room in the mind for anything else. It becomes a very focused moment with God.

"You may say a prayer. You may say a mantra with intention. You can invite God to join you and ask God to be with you, or you can sit and wait for God's Words to come to you. You might ask questions and wait for answers. You may talk to God as if you were telling a dear friend how much you appreciate them in your life and all that they have done for you and given you. You may experience your gratitude for God's Presence and just wallow in thankfulness. You may ask the Holy Spirit or Jesus to communicate with you.

"You will be receiving Truth in all of those forms, in whatever way you can hear God's Message. Continue to invite It. Continue to seek It. Continue to receive It. And know that you are having that connection regardless of what your conscious experience might be. You may hear words. You may see images. You may think certain thoughts that are incredibly loving, inspiring, and filled with Truth. You may have a physical experience. The more that you engage in this, the more you will recognize how it is that *you* hear God. You will become clearer about what it is you are receiving and in what ways, and you will begin to understand the best ways for you to hear God. What are the most powerful, impacting, meaningful, or simplest ways for *you*?

"Perhaps you might begin with starting your day or ending your day with God, and then eventually both. Having more time devoted to this practice will help you become familiar with the process and comfortable with the connection, and eventually you will hear and understand more. You will receive guidance and direction throughout the day that will be more obvious to you, and you will have more overall peace, faith, and trust in your life. Eventually there will be less seeking of guidance and direction because you will just know and understand that everything is perfect. Eventually, this communion begins to stretch between the mornings and the evenings and the times during the day and it begins to fill in the gaps between those set-aside times, so that more and more you are having this communion within your mind, this experience of God, the words, the feelings, the guidance, the direction, and the love. As you take that into more moments of your day, it will one day fill in all of the gaps so that all you have is communication and communion with God and that will become your reality, and the illusion of the world will fall away."

DavidPaul: What is the advantage to hearing words from God versus experiencing God in myriad other ways?

Holy Spirit: "If it isn't broken, don't fix it. If one is experiencing God and has a full, complete, and rewarding relationship with God, they are not seeking more. This book is not for them. It is for people who would like to hear God. These might even be people who have had experiences with God, have felt God, have known God, and yet they can't maintain it or they can't attain it whenever they seek it. They are striving toward that relationship.

"For so many in a humanly form, it is difficult to project onto God that God can be anything other than some type of grand humanly form. The way that humans communicate is with words, primarily. Of course there are actions, deeds, expressions, looks, and so on, though the most abundant type of communication between human forms is talking. Humans love to talk. Therefore, it is imagined that God is a talker also. When you have this concept of God, and it is difficult to have a different one being in a human form yourself, you therefore seek the type of communication you're comfortable and familiar with. It is not that there is an advantage to one over the other, only that if your relationship with God is not everything you want it to be, then the Reality that every single person has God's Voice within them and can access that Voice if they want to is a wonderful reminder and a wonderful gift. This book is not suggesting that everyone should do this, only that everyone *could* if they so desire."

Steps

1. Sit alone in a quiet place where there are no distractions.

2. Connect with God using whatever meditation practice you feel most comfortable with.

3. After a period of time, once the voice of the ego has faded and you experience a strong connection with God, begin a conversation with God, either in your mind or out loud, whichever you prefer. Share with God your intentions, your fears, your hopes and dreams, or anything else you want to share.

4. When you are done communicating what is in your heart, sit quietly and listen for God's Voice. God *will* communicate back to you. If a loving thought comes to you or you think of a loving word or phrase, you are hearing God's Voice. Allow yourself to receive those thoughts or words, and allow them to continue. You are hearing God's Voice within you.

5. If after a few minutes you do not hear or sense anything, imagine moving the radio tuner within your mind to God's Station, to the frequency of the Holy Spirit.

6. Be open to however God's Voice may sound. It might sound like a faint thought or idea. It might sound like a whisper, or it might sound like a wise version of your own inner voice.

7. If you are still unaware of hearing God's Voice, you might allow God's Voice to speak through you. Open your mouth with this intention and

allow yourself to speak God's Words. Allow whatever comes through to come through, no matter what it sounds like…repeating words, broken sentences, the same sentences over and over, or the most beautiful words you have ever heard. It doesn't matter. When you give God a voice, you give yourself the opportunity to receive God's Voice.

8.   For some people, it is difficult to sit and hear God's Voice. You may need to get up and walk with a certain intention or mindfulness. As you walk, go through the process of inviting God to join with you and then allow yourself to hear God's Voice. Keep your mind on God so that whatever is happening around you is irrelevant. Allow the Words to come to you and through you.

DavidPaul: Allowing ourselves to hear and speak God's Voice can be a frightening experience. It's natural to feel incredibly vulnerable, uncertain, or afraid in the moment that we make this commitment and open our mouth. We too have felt this way on many occasions. In these moments, ask the Holy Spirit to help you let go of any fear or uncertainty so that you can open your mouth and hear this Voice within you. You may hear only a few words or thoughts, or you may hear the most Truthful and loving communication you have ever heard. Regardless of what you hear, the more you connect with this Voice, the louder It becomes.

A big part of coming to hear the Holy Spirit in my life was the result of acknowledging where and how I *was* hearing this Voice. By learning to validate my ability to hear the Holy Spirit through signs, for example, the beliefs about my inability to hear this Voice began to change. And as I practiced and learned how to acknowledge and hear the Holy Spirit in other ways, I began to see that I didn't have to hear this Voice in my head to experience and believe that I could hear the Holy Spirit. Eventually, these others ways of hearing became so fulfilling that my need to hear the Holy Spirit in a particular way, i.e. as an audible Voice within me, soon disappeared. Even though I wasn't hearing this Voice how I originally thought I would, these ways of hearing were so rich and rewarding that in my experience, I *was* hearing the Holy Spirit in my life.

It was this conviction and *Reality* that ultimately led to my first experience of hearing the Holy Spirit as a clear and discernible Voice within me. So as you practice hearing the Holy Spirit in various ways, validate yourself and the successes that you have. As your validation builds and builds, you will literally create the perception, experience, and belief that you *are* hearing this Voice in your life. And once this perception takes root, hearing God's Voice in other ways will naturally unfold.

What Does God's Voice Sound Like To Us?

Candace: When I first heard the Holy Spirit, it was an unexpected surprise. It was as if a flood gate had been opened in my mind and waves of communication came rushing in. It reminded me of what it might be like to lose your voice for a long time and finally get it back. There was enthusiasm and passion in the Words I heard and almost an urgency in their delivery. The Words were so loving and beautiful and comforting, and they felt so good to hear.

I talked with this Voice throughout the entire first day, and for several days thereafter, asking questions and learning more about Who and What It was. I didn't know much about the Holy Spirit at the time so it was all new to me. When I would drift off into other thoughts, I would hear the Voice calling me to come back. I would immediately tune back into the Voice and reconnect with this ongoing conversation.

I remember interviewing for a job as a hospice counselor during those first few days. Because I was so connected with this Voice, I was able to hear It over whatever else was going on. I took this Voice into the interview and used It to answer questions about how I would handle a variety of situations involving death and dying. With the help of the Holy Spirit, I answered these questions to the surprise and disbelief of the interviewers. My responses were so filled with Truth and deep acceptance and peace around the topic that the interviewers said they could not hire me because I was too comfortable with death, and in thinking that death was not possible, I would not be a good counselor. Of course from their perspective, this was true. I, on the other hand, thought I would have been a great counselor.

Shortly thereafter, the Voice began to fade and the sounds of the world began to get louder and louder. It was around this time that my good friend, and now husband, sent someone to me to receive communication from the Holy Spirit and thus began the process of hearing this Voice for others, and ultimately for me. This soon became the usual way I heard the Holy Spirit.

When I first began to hear the Words "on command," meaning to share Them with others at a specific time rather than hear Them spontaneously within myself, it was a big leap of faith for me. I'm not sure now why I thought I could do this, but it just seemed to unfold that way. When I first began to do this, I would hear, "You are loved and you are whole." This became almost like a password between me and the Holy Spirit so that I would know I was connected. Over time, the password became unnecessary and the sessions would begin with, "Greetings and blessings to you, precious one(s)." This greeting continues to this day and is always comforting and reassuring to hear.

The first dozen or so times that I shared God's Voice with others, I would literally read the Words on a screen in my mind. It was as if They were being slowly typed, and I would read Them out loud. There was no time delay between seeing the Words and speaking Them so I wasn't able to think before I spoke. As an individual session with someone went on, the Words would come faster and I would begin to grasp what the Message was really about.

With each subsequent session, the Words came faster and faster, until one day they stopped appearing in front of me and I just heard Them. At first, I would hear a line and then convey that line, hear another line and then convey that line. Eventually, the Words came through with no delay between hearing Them and speaking Them and the style became much more conversational. Sometimes the Holy Spirit would joke with people and tease them playfully in ways I never would have imagined.

When the Words began to flow freely with others, I started to see a movie in my head of what was being said. Sometimes I would see a picture, but mostly I would see a movie playing and that would tell me more about what was going on than the Words themselves. Sometimes the movie would allow me to see the bigger picture of what was being said. Other times, it showed me details that weren't mentioned otherwise and I would sometimes have a different sense of the Message.

The sessions I did with others were primarily about teaching them how to hear this Voice for themselves. The Holy Spirit told me early on that my agreement with the Holy Spirit was to help teach others how to hear God's Voice. I didn't sign up to be a go between, but rather to inspire others and demonstrate this Gift from God. When I asked, "Why me?" the Holy Spirit told me that I was a good example for people because anyone who knew me would say, "If she can do it, anybody can!"

When I hear the Holy Spirit now, It is not something I hear in my head, so much as a Voice that comes out when I open my mouth to share It. When I do hear the Holy Spirit in my head, It sounds like an old friend talking to me. I have to concentrate deeply to stay tuned in to the Voice and the Words flow into me as if I'm sitting with a trusted partner. To this day, I sometimes have doubts that something will come through me when I open my mouth or that what I say will make no sense. But I keep opening my mouth with the faith I have gained from many years of practice, knowing that whatever happens will be perfect.

———————

DavidPaul: When I first heard the Voice of the Holy Spirit that morning with Candace, It didn't sound like I thought it would. For years, I imagined It would be like talking on the phone or hearing a loud Voice within me, but when it actually happened, there was no separate or distinct Voice. I was hearing the Words for the first time as I was speaking Them out loud. At first, I didn't think it was really happening, that maybe I was somehow making it up, but when I heard the Words coming out of my mouth, I could feel the Holy Spirit within Them, and I knew They weren't mine.

This is the closest description I can think of to share what it is like to hear the Voice of the Holy Spirit within me: Imagine standing in front of a group of your closest friends. One of them suddenly says, "Tell us a story about a grasshopper and a bumblebee." And before you have a chance to think, someone else yells, "Go!" and you have to start speaking immediately without knowing how it's going to start, what's going to be said next, or where the story is going to go. You just have to open your mouth and start speaking...so you do. Within moments, the story begins to take on a life of its own, and you too begin to listen to the story coming out of your mouth. Surprisingly, it's interesting, intriguing, and enjoyable to listen to, and before you know it, you're just as excited as everyone else to see where the story will end. Finally, the story ends and your friends give you a standing ovation. It was a brilliant story, and you agree. You don't know how you pulled it off, but you did, and you're grateful for it.

When I first started hearing this Voice, I heard It only during meditation, while my eyes were closed. As my confidence grew, I began to experiment. First, I practiced doing it with my eyes open. Then I started doing it as I walked through the park near our house. While I walked, I would feel the Holy Spirit's Presence within me and all around me, and when I was ready, I would ask the Holy Spirit to speak to me. I would then open my mouth and start speaking. When people walked by, I would pause, smile, and then start speaking once again. This quickly became my favorite way of hearing the Holy Spirit because the Words seemed to come very easily and naturally when I walked.

Over time, I began to experiment with saying the Words silently to myself instead of saying Them out loud, as if I were reading a book or silently talking to myself. I first started doing this in the morning while lying in bed, not wanting to wake up Candace by talking out loud. I then started doing it around other people, like at the gym or in other public places. At first, I was easily distracted by everyone around me, but the more I practiced, the easier it became.

To this day, whether I'm speaking the Words out loud or silently to myself, I still have to physically form the Words in some way. Even if I'm not speaking the Words out loud, I can still feel my throat and tongue moving as I silently say the Words. I've always wanted to hear this Voice without having to form the Words myself, but I've never experienced that.

One day, I was feeling frustrated about the way I heard the Holy Spirit and wanted to understand why I couldn't hear a more distinctive Voice within me, so I decided to ask the Holy Spirit for some insight. This is what I heard:

Holy Spirit: "Greetings and blessings to you, precious one. Indeed it is a joyous occasion to gather together with you in this way. There are no specific ways that God seeks to speak to His children. He has no goals or preferences for how He speaks. He speaks however His children are able to best hear Him. He speaks to them in ways they are able to receive and in ways that serve them in their growth and in their awareness of their Union with Him.

"You are one who seeks to know your Oneness with God this lifetime. To perceive a separation between His Voice and yours would not support this goal in the way you might think. To always experience His Voice, His Words, and His Thoughts to be separate from your own, to be different in such a way that you can point to Them and find Them and experience Them as different from your own voice, does not serve you.

"There are many who would benefit from this way of hearing God's Voice. There are many who would use this way of hearing to further their awareness of their Oneness with God. Eventually, their experience of Oneness would evolve, and as it did, so would their experience of hearing. Relationship is not a static experience. Your relationship with God, with yourself, and with the world is constantly changing, as is your communication. Even if you were to hear God's Voice as separate, over time, your communication with God would evolve and grow and change.

"You hear and experience God's Voice within you as your Highest Self, the part of your mind that is already connected to God-Mind, the part of your mind that you feel and know to be You, which is also connected with Truth and with God. It is here where God communicates with you, and it is here within yourself that God's Voice is heard. This is always the case, and yet it can be perceived differently by different people. There are many who do not yet experience that aspect of their Self, do not yet know that part of their Self, and are not yet connected and aware of that aspect of their Mind. For them, they experience these Words and these Thoughts to be separate, and yet, in Truth, they can never be separate.

"You were already connected and feeling this part of yourself and knowing this part of yourself when you started hearing God's Voice. It is because of this that you did not experience this Voice as separate from your own, as separate from your mind. As each person awakens to this Voice, he or she will experience It differently, hear It differently, and relate to It in their own unique way. As you have mentioned before, 6 billion people, 6 billion ways. Know that you hear God's Voice in just the right way for you, just as another hears It in just the right way for them.

"Blessings to you precious one. Amen."

DavidPaul: To this day, my hearing of the Holy Spirit continues to grow and strengthen, and I still experiment with where, when, and how I can more fully hear this Voice in my life. Although it's only been a few years since I first started hearing the Holy Spirit in this way, I am repeatedly amazed with what I hear and how it has impacted my life. I can only imagine what it will be like with another fifty or so potential years of practice ahead of me....

Practice

Holy Spirit: "Joining with the Holy Spirit and hearing this Voice is similar to exercise. You can talk about exercise all you want, but until you go to the gym and get on a machine, lift some weights, or start a class, nothing happens. It is the same with hearing the Voice of the Holy Spirit. You can talk about it all you want, and yet if you don't sit down and make that connection, it is only a theory. It is a tool that sits in the toolbox, though you can't remember where the toolbox is or whether you even have the tool, so it doesn't get used when you need it or want it."

———

DavidPaul: For 9 years, we joined with the Holy Spirit for church every Sunday morning wherever we were. This became our primary time as a couple to officially turn off the phones, meditate, hear this Voice, and seek guidance. To better maintain our connection with the Holy Spirit throughout the week, we were eventually guided to check in together at least once during the week as well.

With a regular practice of connecting in this way, the communications we received deepened and the messages would often build upon one another from one week to the next. The Holy Spirit would frequently give us homework assignments and tasks, and we would often share our "successes and failures" with one another and the Holy Spirit the following week. This practice of connecting with the Holy Spirit on a regular basis greatly supported us in moving through many ingrained and dysfunctional patterns in our relationship and in our lives. The more we checked in, the more grace-filled our lives became.

If you don't consciously experience hearing the Holy Spirit in your life, be patient and keep trying. Developing more awareness of it could happen when you least expect it. It's different for everyone because we each have our own unique set of thoughts and beliefs that keep us from hearing this Voice as we would like. For me, it took years of practice, persistence, and faith to finally open up to hearing this Voice within me. It is only now, after several years of hearing It, that I can honestly say that I *was* hearing this Voice all along and didn't know it. So even if you don't think you are hearing It, have faith that you *are* hearing this Voice in one way or another. Keep practicing. And know that the more you choose to hear this Voice, the louder It becomes.

Holy Spirit: "Opening to God's Voice is similar to pipes and faucets that have not been used in some time. It takes a while to crank the handle and eventually get it to open. Air and rust and other things will begin to emerge, followed by some drops of water, and eventually a flow of water. The water will be dirty at first, but after a while the water will run clear and the faucet will become easier and easier to turn on and off.

"This is analogous to hearing God's Voice in that it has just been some time since one has truly given themselves the gift of just listening, opening that faucet and allowing the clear and cold water to run through. Be patient as the bubbles and the rust make their way through the pipes. Continue each day to spend some time joining with God and listening to His Voice. Spend as much time as you can and know that your pipes will open up for you."

Developing Trust and Faith

DavidPaul: Holy Spirit, how does one come to trust that they are hearing God's Voice?

Holy Spirit: "It's different for everyone—six billion people, six billion ways of coming to trust It. For Candace, it was very simple. She knew the Words she heard were not her own. They were so loving and kind and felt so true that she immediately trusted.

"For her, it has taken time, practice, faith, consistency, and more practice to be able to continue with that trust. Even if one has an experience like hers that was very opening and immediately offered trust, that trust has to be maintained, just as it does in any relationship. In the beginning of a relationship, two people may start out trusting each other; they are innocent until proven guilty. That trust has to continually be earned, proven, honored, respected, and so on throughout the length of the relationship. That is done one-sided or two. One can trust another regardless of what the other one does, and two parties may trust each other based on their actions and behaviors.

"For Candace, the process of trust has continued with the opportunity to share this Voice with countless people and have them return each time saying, 'Thank you. That rang so true,' 'Thank you. That was just what I needed to hear,' or 'Thank you. That was exactly right for me.' As this one continues to deliver Messages that serve people, the trust is deepened and strengthened each time. In addition to that, the trust and faith are there each time this one agrees to share this Voice, and every single time that she opens her mouth and that Voice comes through, that trust is reestablished and reconfirmed once again.

"It is the same as being in relationship with anyone. In some cases, trust may not be granted freely in the beginning. Trust may have to be earned from the start, and it may be that as one person engages in a relationship with the Holy Spirit, they ask God and the Holy Spirit to help them trust that Voice, the communication, and the consistency with which It is available to them, which is unending. They can ask for trust. They can pray for trust. They can hold a belief in trust within their heart and mind.

"What often happens in a typical relationship is that trust is broken at some point. From one person's beliefs, thoughts, and understanding of the world to the other person's actions, words, deeds, miscommunications, misunderstandings, etc, confusion reigns and trust dissolves. That is the kind of relationship that people in the world are used to. It is as if one goes into any and all relationships with the understanding that eventually they will be burned. Eventually their trust will be broken. Eventually, somehow, this person will betray them or hurt them. That can only happen from one's thinking, and yet that is what will manifest it.

"So when entering into a relationship with God, the Holy Spirit, and Jesus, it is unlike any other relationship that one has ever entered into, though in Truth, one has never been out of that relationship. As one re-enters that particular relationship, it is so unlike anything they have ever experienced because they will not be betrayed. They will not be burned. They will not be let down. The trust will not ever be compromised, and that, in and of itself, is something that is hard to fathom for so many. It seems inconceivable, impossible, and why even dream about it when it is so unlikely.

"What one must know entering into this relationship is that there can be nothing but trust. There can be nothing but Truth, Reality, clarity, and understanding, and as long as what you continue to hear when you seek God's Voice is loving, caring, truthful, and real, you can know that that is God's Voice speaking to you. If you hear something that is unloving, unkind, or untruthful, you can know that is not God's Voice talking to you. It is the same when you pick up the phone and the other person says 'hello' and you know who it is. It could be anyone calling and you know who it is from that one word. You recognize the voice. It is the same with God's Voice. You will come to recognize that Voice in such a way that there will be no doubt. There will be no confusion, and then the Words will only back up what you know, that this is loving and truthful and real. It must be God's Voice.

"It may start with little things. It may start with big elaborate communications. It doesn't matter. The more time you spend with that Voice, the more time you spend hearing, taking in, and applying what you hear, watching how your life benefits, seeing how your peace of mind grows, how your heart opens, and how your mind empties will become proof for you that what you are hearing is God's Voice.

"Trust is a tricky issue, and it all comes from within you, ultimately. If you can give yourself the gift of trusting, you give that gift to you. It is not what you give to the other person. You do not trust them for their sake. You trust them for yours. In doing so, you will have a relationship that is trustworthy. Whatever belief you hold about what and who they are, that is what you will get.

"You trust in the relationship. You trust in the Voice. You trust in Its willingness and desire and passion to come to you. You trust that God wants to share Truth with you. You trust that this Voice is always available to you. You trust that It is loving and kind, and that is what you will receive. In any moment that it isn't, you stop, take a breath, and simply let go of whatever thoughts have been in your heart and mind just a moment before and you reconnect with what you know is God. You reconnect with what you know is God's Voice, and you ask that only God's Words come to you, and you wait quietly and patiently for those Words to fill you."

DavidPaul: What is the difference between trust and faith?

Holy Spirit: "One has the memory inside of them that in fact they are One with God. It is because of that memory that one knows in their heart that God is. It is because of that memory that they believe in God, remember God, can hear God, and that God can hear them. It is innate because it just *is* the Truth. You cannot take that Truth out of this aspect of God, like the expression that one cannot take the country out of the cowboy. You cannot take God out of that aspect of God. It is an inalienable right. It is your inheritance. It is your heritage, and so It is yours.

"Beyond that, you will have the thoughts that there is no God, you cannot hear, and so forth—that is the ego doing its job and it does not change the basic Truth of what you are. The Truth of what you are does not change, nor can the ego ever take that away from you. So while you may have moments of confusion, the basic foundation is always there, and that is what drives you toward that connection.

"The difference between trust and faith is that with trust, you believe, and with faith, you know. They are very similar but one is stronger. Faith is knowing that the person you are in relationship with is a Child of God. Even if you do not understand what they are doing or saying in that moment, you have faith, which is the memory and the awareness that the one in front of you is a Child of God, as are you, and that, in fact, they could not harm you in any way; they are not capable of it, nor are you capable of being harmed. When you take that faith out into the world, it is the constant reminder that though you may not be able to understand what is happening, you know it is perfect and that only what is right is unfolding."

Chapter Highlights

"All that one needs in order to hear God's Voice is the desire. If the desire is there, the Voice will be given. That is God's Law."

―――――――

"Everything can be used as a tool or means to hear God. You give everything the meaning that it has, so you can allow anything and everything to serve as your communication with God. It is all a matter of perspective."

―――――――

"You can talk about exercise all you want, but until you go to the gym and get on a machine, lift some weights, or start a class, nothing happens. It is the same with hearing the Voice of the Holy Spirit. You can talk about it all you want, and yet if you don't sit down and make that connection, it is only a theory."

―――――――

"When you take that faith out into the world, it is the constant reminder that though you may not be able to understand what is happening, you know it is perfect and that only what is right is unfolding."

12

Messages From Over the Years

"Every kind thought you have ever had,
and every kind word you have ever spoken,
came from the Holy Spirit."

Holy Spirit: "When one first opens up to hearing the Holy Spirit, it can be, as it was for Candace, a floodgate of communication coming in, or it can be a single word that delivers the message, or pieces of communication that are given here and there. Even though Candace's original experience resembled a floodgate, later, in learning how to put the Words of the Holy Spirit onto paper, it came very slowly and painstakingly. In the beginning, it was a word or a phrase, then a sentence, moving on to a paragraph, and finally a page would come through. This came about with practice, persistence, patience, and diligence, along with a desire to hear God's Voice as well as to share God's Voice. One way to share this Voice was to put It on paper and then pass the paper around."

Candace: Since we first began hearing this Voice, we have received thousands of inspiring Messages from the Holy Spirit. Although the following are but a few, they are a hint as to the variety of communications we have received and how our hearing of this Voice has evolved over the years.

Early Entries From Candace's Notebook

Candace: About a year after I began hearing this Voice, I was guided to connect with the Holy Spirit every morning and write down the Messages that I heard in a notebook. This started out as a slow and challenging exercise, but with every passing day, I got better at hearing, writing, and heeding the messages. Below are the first few entries from my notebook, which show the progression and the types of things I heard.

June 23, 1995
Holy Spirit: "Walk your talk...."

June 24, 1995
Holy Spirit: "Blue.
"No one is at fault when one loses a game. (This comment was made in relation to feeing bad about something that happened the night before.)
"The color blue is a message.
"You are loved.... Know it. Feel it. See it. Speak it. Hear it. Love it. You are loved.
"Amen."

June 25, 1995
Holy Spirit: "Check in more often. Don't wait til later. It is with joy and ease that we have this communication today. It is through your willingness and surrender that this is happening.
"You are lovely and delightful. You may heal yourself through joy, through hope, through failing to remember your sorrows, through victory over your shortcomings (perceived).
"You are one who can know the Truth in all situations but can forget to ask. Trust the guidance you receive. Trust that the guidance you receive is True guidance. You know this in your heart. Settle into it, your heart, and make a place for yourself there. There is always room for you in your heart. Go there child. We love you.
"Amen."

June 26, 1995
Holy Spirit: "Yes, precious one, today we will move in a different direction. Today you will gather puzzle pieces of information from all those around you.

You will gather information from all sources about the direction of your path. It will be up to you to recognize these pieces and make sense of them. Of course, we will help you. This is a lesson in seeing Source in everyone, in hearing Source in everyone, in knowing Source in everyone, in appreciating Source in everyone.

"Get your notebook and begin…. We love you."

June 27, 1995
Holy Spirit: "Aloha, precious one. Surrender deeper. Surrender to Truth, to Knowing, to Love, to Joy, to Peace, to Serenity. It is with Joy (God) that we may have this communication and experience for ourselves the delight in our joining. You did well getting the puzzle pieces yesterday. You also missed quite a few. (Happy face) We had fun. Enjoy, relax, and surrender into your heart's desire. It is there waiting for you and cannot be denied forever.

"Amen."

June 28, 1995
Holy Spirit: "Good morning child. Precious one, you are learning to be connected in every moment. When every experience is a possible puzzle piece to your joy and happiness, it keeps you much more interested. Does it not? You are waking up to your heart's desire. Keep surrendering to it.

"Begin a second notebook. Let this be for your heart's desire and all that that would mean. Let your heart's desire pour out of you into the world to shine light on all your Brothers and Sisters. Bless them with your love. Bless yourself with this love. Go this day and be happy.

"Amen."

Being a Messenger

October 31, 1997
Holy Spirit: "Greetings and blessings to you, precious one. This is a good way to start the day, is it not? Let's begin with a prayer for you to use for these sessions.

'God, may You help me and guide me in all that I do, that I may better work for You. Show me how to align our Wills through this and all that I do. Thank You, Father. Amen.'

"That was tougher than you thought it would be. Perhaps committing to yourself that you won't change anything you are given (meaning the Words of the Holy Spirit) even if it doesn't make sense to you, because it may just be that you are not ready to hear, though you may be someday. If you change it, it is gone forever. It won't be there for you when you need it. It is important to become very clear in your intention for this communication, and how you will receive it. What do you want to accomplish from this?"

Candace: Clear communication with God. A friendship with God. The ability to be loving in every thought, word, and deed. A sense of Servantship that carries me through this lifetime. Peace in my Heart and Mind.

Holy Spirit: "That is a good start. Then what state of Mind/Being would you need to be in to accomplish those goals from this work? Come to it in humility, grace and gratitude rather than thinking about getting it out of the way and getting on with other more important things. Is anything really more important than the goals you have listed here? I can think of nothing. Hold these goals in your mind each day when you begin this work with Us, so that you can be clear as to what is really important to you. Be reminded that nothing else actually matters. Not the laundry, the cleaning, the shopping, the work out, nothing. Only this will bring you peace. We sound like a commercial trying to sell you on a weight loss program, yet use your own discernment to determine what is true for you. We cannot do that for you. We can only state the Truth. Your free will determines what you do with the Truth. May it be with God's Blessings that you do what is truly best for you.

"On with the session…. It would be very good to discontinue the use of the word 'channeling' in your description of what you do. Annie is Mary's Stenographer. What shall you be? A Messenger? 'Please don't kill the messenger,' they say. Perhaps that is why this title has scared you. You feel like a victim when you are the messenger, when, in fact, it is the position of least responsibility. You are not responsible for the message itself, only the delivery of it. You cannot be held accountable for the message. Isn't this a relief? It should be. Rejoice in this freedom, knowing that you have chosen this, you have asked for the opportunity to be a messenger, as there was nothing else you wanted more. Next time we will work on your worthiness for it.

"Have a nice day. We love you Sister, and wish only the best for you. Please do not turn us off today, just because you turn this machine (computer) off.

"The Holy Spirit and your Friend"

Why Am I Here?

November 16, 1997

Holy Spirit: "We love you precious one. We have always loved you; you know that. Be not afraid of these words that come to you in this way. Be not afraid to hear the Truth, for It serves you. Precious one, know that the Truth is in you. Who would you be without your story? A happy person? A contented person? One without the need to make bad choices, be self destructive, create drama? How about just one little soul who fulfills her destiny quietly, peacefully, lovingly, in communion with God—no frills, no glamour, no recognition? Would that be fun? Would it be enough to have a completely fulfilling relationship with God that no one else knew about—just you and God? Perhaps at that time you could teach others how you've done it. To share it before you have understood it, mastered it, accepted it, had it completely, is to give it away before you have owned it.

"Be committed to complete ownership of this experience you have with God, then share it. This will come about in time and with practice and discipline. At this point you are still struggling to have this fully, still struggling with how best to use this Gift. It has been given to you to use for yourself, to hear God so that you can be guided in all situations, not just the obvious and easy ones. This Gift has been given to you to use and experience, then share. It has been given to you so that you can apply it to your life and show others how to do the same. You have had many lifetimes in which hearing God was not a possibility in your mind. You vowed to bring God's Voice into the world this lifetime and use It to the fullest, creating miracle after miracle with It, and in the process inspiring others to find their Voice for God within themselves.

"When you do not use this Voice in your hours of need, you are, in fact, showing others that this Voice is only for the good times, not all times. You are saying that this Voice is only there for you when you are balanced and happy and able to hear It due to your state of being, rather than God's Voice being there for you always, especially when you are uncertain and afraid.

"Continue to ask the question, 'Why am I here?' and continue to get the answer. Let the answer guide you in your life and in your work. You are here for a reason, as are all of God's children. All of His children want to know why they are here, what is their purpose, what is their gift, how do they use their gift to fulfill their purpose. They are only asking these questions because there are answers to them. Everyone has a gift and a purpose...a mission to be performed for God and themselves. Become more and more aware of yours. It is time to begin to fulfill it. We love you!"

Peace

December 8, 1997

Holy Spirit: "Greetings precious one. Good morning. Today is a day of peace for you. A day that you can have to practice peace, perfect peace, being at peace with everything that happens. This means being one or joining with everything. Peace, just like paradise, is a state of being. You can have it anywhere, anytime, anyhow, under any circumstances. That is the beauty of it. You do not have to go anywhere or do anything. It is just yours for the asking, seeking, taking, choosing. Choose peace. It is that simple. Peace over struggle. Peace over pain. Peace over disharmony. It is a tough choice, but you can do it. You can spend this day choosing peace in any and every situation. Peace with yourself, peace in your mind, peace in your interaction with others, peace in every situation. Practice this today and see how simple it really is. Believe it or not, this could become a habit—peace as a way of life.

"You have the concept that peace is indifference or neutrality or not caring, but that is not so. It is acceptance, understanding, and a lack of judgment. This is a deep level of caring, a deep level of love. This is how God loves and how He maintains peace. So if peace came from unconditional love, would it then be worthwhile to love in this way? It would seem so. Practicing peace seems an easier place to begin than practicing unconditional love. Peace takes tremendous will power, for disharmony is what we are used to. Fortunately, peace is our natural state of being, so once it is regained, it is easy to maintain. And it becomes easier to regain again and easier to maintain for longer, then even easier to regain, until finally, you are at peace for good.

"All your little steps are taking you there. The way you are getting there looks different from the way your mate is getting there, but it is the same in Truth. You have each found ways that work for you, and each other's ways do not necessarily work for the other. So they might seem to each of you to not be working at all, when in fact, they are. This is the beauty of it. It is a dance, and a dance worth watching.

"As each one of God's children makes his or her way Home again, they are performing a beautiful dance along the way. That is what keeps us entertained through all of this. Watching the dance is an honor, as it is a beautifully choreographed piece of art that is unfolding in complete Grace and Glory for all to see.

The practice of being in the moment and truly seeing the beauty and the grace of each step is the key. Without that ability, it would sometimes appear to be a stumbling, bumbling lot of moves with no purpose or rhythm. This is why choosing to be present, to be in the moment, and to see through the Eyes of Love and Peace can be so worthwhile. Choose this precious one, and see, truly see, what happens.

"We love you."

Roll in the Mud

February 6, 1998

Holy Spirit: "Greetings precious one. What a glorious day. The heavens have opened up and are blessing you with all of their riches. (It is raining cats and dogs outside.) Just imagine opening your heart and receiving an equivalent amount of Love from God. It *is* possible, and sometimes just as messy. You notice that it is not messy when it leaves the heavens, only when it hits the earth. Why is that? Perhaps the rain is washing away all of the dirt that has accumulated. Perhaps God's Love is washing away all of the Earth-Mind Consciousness that has built up. And in the process of washing away, it looks ugly for a little while. Soon it will be beautiful again, and sooner still it will become dirty.

"Often, one tries to keep something clean and pristine by not using it, thinking that by keeping something in a box or on a shelf it will be preserved. This is to deny oneself the experience of that thing, only later to find that it has been ruined by sitting in a box or on a shelf, and that it would have kept longer if it had been used. And many times things improve with use, especially if they are used lovingly. This 'thing' or 'it' in this case, is one's life. Therefore, do not live cautiously for fear of getting dirty. Live dangerously. Roll in the mud. Play a lot. Mess up your hair. Lose buttons. And know that you get out of your life whatever you put into it.

"Blessings to you. Amen"

Holy Union

February 20, 1998

Holy Spirit: "Precious one, a holy union is a sacred trust. A holy union is different than a union. A holy union means that two people have joined together with God and have agreed to do God's Will in their partnership. The purpose of a holy union is joining with God. You have entered into a holy union, and as such there are responsibilities that go along with this. There is a responsibility to yourself and your partner to experience God in yourself and your partner. There is also a responsibility to experience God in all things so that you may someday know only Love. Your goal in this lifetime is to be only Love. It is therefore essential that you join in holy union so you may come to know and love your self as no other. The most important work you could do this lifetime would be to come to know and love yourself. It is from this that you may know and love another. To live as though everyone on earth were simply a reflection of you would be the highest form of living.

"You have fears that you will not measure up as a partner. The person you need to be a partner to is yourself. You cannot fail in your partnership with DavidPaul. You can only fail in your partnership with yourself. Fortunately, you cannot fail in your partnership with God either. God's experience of your partnership is Perfection. This could be your experience as well. Indeed to know and to love your self is to know and love God, and to feel God's Presence in your heart and mind. This is the ultimate in living.

"We love you and bless you in every way."

In Touch with the Holy Spirit

Candace: People submit questions to the Holy Spirit through our website, and we answer these questions with the Holy Spirit and then post the replies. One day, someone who questioned the content of our website asked if we were really "in-touch" with the Holy Spirit…and if we were, to prove it by telling him his middle name. After reading his e-mail, we received the following communication.

August 1, 1999
Holy Spirit: "Greetings and blessings to you precious ones. Indeed it is a joyous occasion to gather together with you in this way. There are so many reasons for the messages that you would receive via email. Part of those reasons may include validation or recognition. It also includes for you the opportunity to look into any places within yourselves where you have a matching experience with the person who writes to you. So if someone like Joseph asks, 'Are you in touch with the Holy Spirit?' you can ask yourself that question, 'Am I in touch with the Holy Spirit?"

"The question to him is, 'Why is it that *you* doubt *your* connection to the Holy Spirit?' He cannot doubt *your* connection to the Holy Spirit unless he doubts *his* own connection to the Holy Spirit.

"The two of you can also take this opportunity to find a place within yourselves where this may be true to whatever degree. When we join together in this way, there is a connection with the Holy Spirit, of course, and yet in your day-to-day, hour-to-hour, minute-to-minute life, how connected are you? Are you in touch with the Holy Spirit? That is his question, and it simply offers you an opportunity to look deeper into yourselves, to ask certain questions, and to join ever deeper in your communion with the Holy Spirit.

"No physical reactions occurred inside Candace when she read that letter from Joseph, where normally her heart might stop beating or there may be a knot in her stomach for a moment. None of these things occurred. It was that person's experience, and it is not her experience of the Holy Spirit. And she did not even have to react to this projection. At the same time, still ask yourself, 'Are there any places within me where I doubt my connection? Am I in touch?'

"You will be challenged. The more that you put yourselves out there, the more you will be challenged to prove it, the more people will come along and say, 'Tell me my middle name,' as if the Holy Spirit were a psychic. Obviously, there's no need to go there. You are not out to prove anything. At the same time, you want to prove to yourselves your connection with the Holy Spirit, your worthiness for this connection, and your ability to apply this connection under any circumstances. One of Candace's dreams in having this connection was that the whole entire world could come crumbling down around her and she would stand there like a rock and say hello to the Holy Spirit first—not run, not scream, not cry, not panic, but first say hello to the Holy Spirit, to have that connection under the worst of circumstances, to tune-in first and panic later if need be.

"Where within you would you not do that first? As you put yourselves out there more and more, and as you consider writing books and sharing the communication that you've received, you will receive criticism at every turn. You can do whatever you want with this criticism. You can learn from it. You can know yourself better. You can project it back on to the person who gave it to you. You can bless that person for showing you a place within you that you can explore more thoroughly. You can love that person where they are, having nothing to do with you at all, just loving them.

"There are many, many options, and you will be faced with this over and over and over again. You each already know the one response, to be loving to whomever this is occurring. If you cannot do that, then there is no walking the talk of this teaching. In that moment, be loving to the person who is attacking you or ask the Holy Spirit why it is happening. Ask, 'What can I do to shift this?' or be loving in that moment and walk away and ask later. If you say, 'I'm so angry about this and I know the truth of what's really gone on!' you are angry with that person because they have told you something you did not want to hear.

"Do either of you (Candace or DavidPaul) have any questions?"

DavidPaul: Why doesn't the Holy Spirit play prove it with people?

Holy Spirit: "Faith is something that you have. Faith is a desire, a desire to believe. And what you believe *is*. A lack of faith is wanting to not believe. So how many things would you have to say and do to prove to somebody to completely shift and transform them to a place where they become filled with faith? You could spend the rest of your life on one person. They will create what they need to create to develop faith or not. Your job is not to instill faith in them. That is between them and God. Your job is to offer them communication, and it is not to prove to them that they should have faith because this is real or not real. That is *their* life lesson. It may be ten lifetimes or a thousand lifetime lessons. It could not possibly be your job to do that for someone else. Can you see that? Telling someone their middle name will just be a party trick. It has no value. It has no substance. It will not prove anything."

DavidPaul: So what would a good response to him be?

Holy Spirit: "What I told Candace this morning as to his middle name, 'one who lacks faith.' And she was told not to apologize for anything. Candace wanted to say, 'I'm sorry that you're not happy with the response. I'm sorry that you are unable to experience faith,' or whatever it may be. There are no sentences that are to begin with 'I'm sorry,' in this situation. You can speak honestly and straightforwardly to this one and say that as he stated, he is comfortable with his current situation and until the pain and the suffering truly becomes unbearable, he is not motivated to change it. Does that make sense?"

DavidPaul: Yeah.

Holy Spirit: "You can see the benefit to so many people contacting you with their communications, and they are just you in drag, offering you the opportunity to explore in yourselves things that you may take for granted with regard to the Holy Spirit, places you may not want to go, questions you may not want to ask, fears you may not want to acknowledge, doubts you may not want to admit. And these people will offer all of those to you…every last one of them and then some. And that is the beautiful gift that they are."

God's Puzzle

November 18, 1999

Holy Spirit: "It is not life experience that teaches a baby to laugh. She is born with a spark of God, and that part of her remains intact. She is whole in her totality, though God is incomplete without her. This is why each one of His children (sparks of Himself) must return to Him eventually to complete the Giant Puzzle that is Source, and in doing so, each piece will finally feel its completeness. What a happy day that will be. And yet, through the perceptions in one's mind, it would be possible to experience this completeness as having already happened because, in Truth, it has.

"If each of God's children must return to Him to complete the Puzzle, is it not true that you are a piece of that Puzzle? It is not also true then that you have a vested interest in that Puzzle being completed? Does it do you any good to hurry back to Source when nothing can be accomplished until all of the pieces are in place? It is true then that what would do you the most good would be to help the most amount of God's children return Home? This is the way to live.

"If what benefits the whole ultimately benefits you, then serve the whole. And do it lovingly and humbly, knowing that you are only really serving yourself. You are not doing anyone else any favors in Truth. Your call to service, then, is to serve yourself and you do this best by helping everyone along the way get to the same destination with as much Grace and dignity as possible. Can you do this? Are you doing this? How can you do this better?

"Is it not essential then to slow down and see where you could serve yourself at every opportunity? Slow down so that you can notice when you are being called to service. Service can be as small as a smile or as big as a loving thought. It only matters that you are able to be of service to those who are trying to get Home, and that you know you are doing it for yourself rather than for the other person so that there are no debts incurred in the process. How can you do this better? Be aware of this question, asking yourself continually, how can I do this better?"

AOL Stock

January 17, 2000

Holy Spirit: "Greetings and blessings to you, precious ones. Indeed it is a joyous occasion to gather together with you in this way, having church. For Candace, your mind is filled with thoughts and possibilities, potential outcomes. Yes, it is very important for you to be in your own business. You do not have to save anyone or anything, nor are you responsible for anyone or anything other than yourself. Be in your business, allowing the rest of the business to be God's.

"Do you have questions you would like to ask?"

DavidPaul: The AOL Time Warner stock deal. Obviously there is stuff going around in the press that we won't be an Internet company anymore and the stock won't go up as quickly.

Holy Spirit: "It does not matter what occurs with AOL Time Warner, or iPlanet, or anyone else. What matters in your movie is your faith in being able to manifest your dreams and in overcoming your fears. Does that make sense?"

DavidPaul: It is just so hard.

Holy Spirit: "That is the point. We have said previously that between now and living your dream you will overcome your fears. Your goal is to walk away fearless because you know that God is taking care of you. If you think that AOL and what they do is taking care of you, then you are misguided. It is not that you don't love and appreciate AOL and keep them in your prayers. It's only to know and have faith that God is taking care of you. You have said your prayers, made your statement to the universe, and have made a commitment to be a holy family. Between now and that time, all you are doing is letting go of fears. If you have the opportunity now to be complete with your work in two years, it is because you are making progress with your fears and for no other reason. It is not because there was a merger.

"In your movie, your life and everything that happens in it is based on your writing and your directing. As you grow in strength, grow in faith, grow in certainty that what you are asking for is in your highest good and for the highest good of everyone involved, and you know in your heart that God is blessing that, then you can let go of what is between you and that prayer. That is all you would need to live your dream and be a holy family, and yet, you can't get there with the fears and lack of faith. For you to walk away from your company with enough money to live your dream and to have not overcome these issues would be pointless. Having your peace and your happiness come from the numbers in your bank account, and having your faith be in a company, and having your security lie in the stock market, you can see that you would never have peace. This is an opportunity for you to deepen and strengthen your faith, your commitment, your prayers, your desires. That part is your responsibility.

"It is important, essential, and the only thing that matters...the only thing that is True, the only thing that is Real...is to believe in God. Yes, you still validate your company and you show up every day, but that is different than putting your faith, literally your faith in your future, into a company. You can have faith in that company and keep that company in your prayers and in God's Hands knowing that it is the symbol you are using, but your faith has to be in God. So you override the news and the talk at work, and for whatever comes, you give thanks.

"DavidPaul's lesson of the week: Merger.... 'Thanks, God.' Stock goes down.... 'Thanks God.' Lots of fear.... "Thank you, God. I have the opportunity to work on fear.' Lots of celebration.... "Thank you, God. I have the opportunity to celebrate this next step toward living my dream, which is really a step in deepening my faith in God.' Whatever comes.... 'Thank you, God.' It is all in God's Hands, and your faith in God is what will allow you to leave AOL and pursue your dreams, not your faith in AOL.

"Anything could happen to AOL; nothing could happen to God. If something were to happen to AOL and you have faith in God and your prayers and desires, God will take care of you. Only something better can happen. It is putting the cart before the horse. You cannot trust this process until you can trust this process, and yet that is the point of this process. We will work on this over and over and over again. There will come a time when you will be as free of this as one can be, so that even when you become burdened by this, you will know it is just your lack of faith in God rather than an earthly fear. To put your faith in AOL is to build your house on sand. To have your faith in God and use AOL as a symbol is to build your house on rock."

Chapter Highlights

"Continue to ask the question, 'Why am I here?' and continue to get the answer. Let the answer guide you in your life and in your work.... Everyone has a gift and a purpose...a mission to be performed for God and themselves. Become more and more aware of yours. It is time to begin to fulfill it."

———

"As each one of God's children makes his or her way Home again, they are performing a beautiful dance along the way.... The practice of being in the moment and truly seeing the beauty and the grace of each step is the key."

———

"...do not live cautiously for fear of getting dirty. Live dangerously. Roll in the mud. Play a lot. Mess up your hair. Lose buttons. And know that you get out of your life whatever you put into it."

———

"The most important work you could do this lifetime would be to come to know and love yourself. It is from this that you may know and love another. To live as though everyone on earth were simply a reflection of you would be the highest form of living."

———

"If each of God's children must return to Him to complete the Puzzle, is it not true that you are a piece of that Puzzle? It is not also true then that you have a vested interest in that Puzzle being completed? Does it do you any good to hurry back to Source when nothing can be accomplished until all of the pieces are in place? It is true then that what would do you the most good would be to help the most amount of God's children return Home?"

Part III
Living With God's Voice

———

"The Light that I am lights your way,
which lights my way, which lights your way,
which lights my way."

———

13

Seeking God's Voice in the World

"How I see is a choice.
I can see the world or I can see Heaven,
and the scenery doesn't change."

Holy Spirit: "When one seeks God's Voice in the world, they are seeking Truth. They are seeking a perspective that is Right-Minded and offers a way of seeing things from a new light. When one seeks God's Voice in the world, they give themselves the opportunity to see things from a perspective that offers them peace, joy, and the reminder of who they truly are. They give themselves the gift of seeing the world through God's Eyes—in whatever way and to whatever degree they are willing. The Words they hear may sound different to each one, and yet they will be given Truth every time."

DavidPaul: Hearing God's Voice has the potential to bring us peace when we are in pain, clarity when we are confused, and understanding when we do not know. Over the years, we have received countless questions from visitors to our website asking the Holy Spirit for communication and guidance in times of need. The following examples illustrate how the Holy Spirit speaks to each of us exactly where we are and how hearing this Voice offers a way of perceiving ourselves, the world, and everything in it from a new perspective.

161

Fear of a Broken Heart

Maggie: Holy Spirit, I am in the process of getting divorced and have met a very wonderful man who touches my soul. I am scared of a relationship because of a fear of not being perfect, and my main fear is that of a broken heart. I am wondering how this relationship will work out and how I should handle it so that no feelings will be hurt. I want to be with this man. Will I be? Will it be a forever relationship? Thank you.

Holy Spirit: "Greetings and blessings to you precious one. You ask how to have this relationship without any feelings being hurt. Well, you will have to roll yourself up in cotton batting, lock yourself up in a closet and not have contact with anyone or anything, and then not allow your mind to think any thoughts. Perhaps then, with a little luck, you may not have your feelings hurt, and yet, even that is probably not possible.

"So, with the prospect of beginning a relationship, what you must do is expect and look forward to the opportunity to have your feelings hurt so that you can come to know yourself better, know the areas where you are challenged, and pray that those places become healed and whole and filled with faith and love rather than fear, as they are now. To have a fear of your heart breaking will allow you first and foremost to focus on your heart breaking rather than to focus on your heart opening and allowing more love, more joy, and more capacity for love to be within you.

"The fear of a broken heart is what will create a broken heart. Nothing else can actually do it. You can be abandoned, abused, violated, unloved, rejected, and none of that need cause you to have a broken heart; it is how you handle the situation that will or will not cause you to experience having a broken heart. You can also have lots of love, support, and kindness in your life and still walk around believing that your heart is broken or will be broken. It is strictly your perspective and your experience of this situation that will cause you to have a broken heart or not.

"To want to be with this man is one thing and to have it be what is best for you may be something different altogether. For you, the most important thing is to pray only for that which is in your highest good and to avoid the prayers that specifically ask to be with this person forever. You cannot focus on or worry about the future. It is something that is ever-changing based on your own evolution and where you are in your life. Something may be perceived as forever and then you could shift your perspective in an afternoon and change the course of your life entirely. The future is not important; it is the now that is important.

How do you perceive now? How do you love now? How open are you now to that which is for your highest good? Allow yourself to pray for peace and openness within your own heart so that you can receive and give love in the ways that you truly desire. That is your birthright, and if you truly want it, it will be done.

"Blessings to you precious one. Amen."

Am I Doing the Right Thing?

Joanne: Holy Spirit, my fiancé and I just broke up, and I need to know if this was the right thing to do or not. I love him more than anything else in the whole world. We were planning on being married in April. I just felt like he put himself above me in his priorities. He would make plans with me and then go play golf instead, or he would simply forget to call because something more important came up. I love him and miss him very much, but I feel like maybe it's best for us to be apart until he can change this selfish aspect of his personality. Should I be patient and stick it out or move on?

Holy Spirit: "Greetings and blessings to you precious one. To say that this person has a tendency to be selfish and to have the idea that you can change his personality, or that *he* can, is perhaps not very realistic. What is more realistic in making a lifetime commitment to someone is to make a commitment to who that person is in their entirety, to accept the things about them that you cannot change, and even different than that, to accept everything about them as potentially something that can never be changed—that who you know and see before you now is the person you will spend everyday of your life with. It is important to marry who is standing in front of you today and to not marry them for who you think they will become or to not marry them for who you are afraid they might turn into. It is the one in front of you who is real and who you would be spending your days with.

"If you cannot live with the selfishness of this person now, it may only be magnified over days, weeks, months, or years in a marriage. Can you imagine yourself in this relationship with these tendencies multiplying over time? Or can you see yourself making peace with this and not having this person's selfishness impact you? Are you strong enough to not be affected by this person's selfishness? Or would you rather make a lifetime commitment to someone who does not have selfish tendencies? If this person is selfish with you, what will they be like with your family, your children, or over a lifetime?

"This is an opportunity for you to do some soul-searching. If you experience this person as selfish, in what ways does his selfishness make you uncomfortable because you are selfish? What kinds of things about yourself would you like to change? What types of things about you would you like to experience differently? In what ways would you like to be different in a relationship? It is important for you to focus on you and to focus less on this person, their flaws, and the changes that they should make. Take this time to focus on you. What shifts can you make so that you like you better? In doing so, you will come to like yourself in such a way that you will attract and keep someone who equally likes themselves and who is equally committed to knowing themselves and working toward being the best person they can be.

"Have faith that this process is one that is serving you in every way. Blessings to you precious one. Amen."

Overcoming Addiction

Cheryl: I am having trouble letting go of an over the counter addiction and smoking. I really need the Holy Spirit to guide me and strengthen me so I can overcome these things.

Holy Spirit: "Greetings and blessings to you precious one. To want to give up the addictions you are speaking of is, of course, the first and biggest step. To know that there are things that you are doing that are not serving you is the most important awareness that can happen to shift addictions. At the same time, it creates pain because you suddenly become aware that this is not something that is serving you, and yet you are still doing it. There is a time lag between the awareness that what you are doing is causing you pain and the inability to stop doing it. Know that once you get to the other side, there will be tremendous peace, and yet you can still have peace in this process knowing that your awareness has taken you to the first and the biggest step in changing something you are unhappy with.

"There will be a time when these addictions will be behind you and you will have the blessing of addiction in your experience and the strength and the confidence that comes from overcoming it. You will then be able to encourage and inspire others as well. This transition period is painful, confusing, paradoxical, and at the same time exciting and very door opening.

"It is important to be patient, to be loving, and to be kind and accepting with yourself right now. Battling, fighting, and abusing yourself to give up something such as an addiction is not the best way, although it is often the most common way. Be patient and kind and know that for you, the more that you love yourself, the more you can let go of these things that do not serve you.

"Spend time each day consciously noticing yourself, admiring yourself, loving yourself, thinking about what it is about you that you like, that makes you special, that you want to share with others, and that you wish others knew about you. Focus on those things and experience them within your heart and mind. Experience the love that you have for yourself. You do have tremendous love within you, though for you it is just buried, confused, and doubtful at times. Underneath all of that, there is a very deep and abiding love that you have for you. That love is what will carry you through this process.

"The more you love you, the more you cannot do the things that do not serve you. The more you love you, the less room there is for anything other than that which is good. Spend more time loving you and there will be less room for these addictions. It is truly that simple. Eventually, you will run out of room within you to do those things that do not serve you. Love yourself and have faith that this day is coming.

"Blessings to you precious one, Amen."

My Fairy Tale Is Gone

John: Holy Spirit, my girlfriend and I recently split up. I called her a few days ago and she said that it was over, that I had gotten on her nerves to the point where she didn't see any point in communicating with me anymore—ever. I told her I was completely devastated. She said, "I know, but that happens to people everyday and you need to act like an adult for once."

I just don't understand what happened. I am so hurt and confused and lonely. I bought her flowers almost every week we dated and treated her like a princess. I cry and pray every day for her to return. How can I get my fairy tale back?

Holy Spirit: "Greetings and blessings to you, precious one. What is attractive about a person is their character, their strengths, their goals, their beliefs. In some cases, it may be external things, and yet, for the most part, it is who they are and all of the richness they bring into the world and share with another. That is what you brought to this relationship in the first place. Who you became over time was a person who is in love with this other person, rather than a man of character, virtue, ideas, and goals. You lost who you were in the process of this relationship, and you lost what made you desirable to her in the first place.

"You have not done anything wrong or bad. This happens naturally for people in relationships when they are not strong and certain about who they are and about their character and strengths. Those become lost in the course of a relationship. For you, it would be best to allow your fairy tale to read onto the next page where it says, 'And they lived happily ever after. The End.' You close the book and say, 'That was a nice story. God bless those characters.' And you move on.

"Give thanks in your heart for having known this person and for having learned that in the course of falling deeply and wonderfully in love, you lose yourself. Then go about your life, without this person, rediscovering your strengths, your character, your virtues and goals. Focus on these and strengthen these. They are already instilled within you in a very deep way. Make contact with those things on the deepest level that you can, so that you bring them into the world and into your relationships, rather than bringing your neediness, your dependence, or your suffering, which came as a result of losing yourself in this relationship.

"Rediscover within you all of these things. When you feel strong and confident in who you are, bring that into the world and allow another relationship to unfold in your life, being mindful not to lose yourself in the process. It is not to be self-centered when you step into a relationship, but to continue to make yourself, your relationship with God, your family, your work, your goals, and your priorities as important as they truly are.

"You have everything within you that you need to accomplish this. It is only for you to make the decision and take the time to do this. Allow yourself to be motivated to maintain who you are and to allow your partner to maintain who they are so that the relationship becomes the blessing of the gifts that you each bring, knowing that you are stronger as a couple than the sum of your parts.

"Blessings to you on this happy venture. Amen."

A Secret to Share

Maria: Holy Spirit, I have been through a lot over the last 3 years. I have divorced, suffered from cancer, and started a new relationship with someone I care a great deal about. One of my problems is that I have been trained professionally to be a very secretive person. I have kept things and told lies to this person because of my secretiveness. Needless to say, it has created problems in this relationship. I know that this is wrong, but when you are trained this way, it is a hard habit to break. I worked undercover for several years so you can see where this is coming from. I don't want to be like this. Please pray for me and give me some insight as to how I can break this habit. Thank you.

Holy Spirit: "Greetings and blessings to you precious one. Indeed it is a joyous occasion to gather together with you in this way. Thank you for your request of prayers and guidance.

"It is one thing to say that your secretiveness comes as a result of the work you have done, but it may be true that you chose the work you did out of a desire to be secretive. Which came first, the chicken or the egg? In your case you have been protecting yourself and doing your best to avoid being hurt any more than you have already been hurt. You have created the idea that to be secretive, to close down, or to hide is the best way you know to protect yourself. This keeps you from letting someone in, and it keeps you from being able to come out. There is the fear that if one were to know you completely, they would not like you or love you. There is the fear that if you love or that if you are loved, you will ultimately be hurt.

"There are many ways to experience life's lessons. Every experience can teach you something, yet the same experience might teach ten people ten different things. If one reaches into their oven to take something out and they are burned, one person might say that reaching into a hot oven will cause you to be burned. Another person would say to use your oven mitts when reaching into a hot oven to prevent getting burned. Another person may decide that baking is dangerous and they give it up altogether. Some people might think that they had been stupid and deserved to be burned. You can see that the same experience can offer people many different conclusions. You have had certain experiences and based on those you came to believe that it is better to hide and better to not love or be loved. Those conclusions do not need to be your truths any longer.

"The real truth is that it is not safe to *not* love or be loved because if you do not love or are not loved, surely you will perish. If you think it is better to hide so that one cannot know you and have the opportunity to not like you, you also close the door to the opportunity for someone to like you for who you really are. The key here is for you to break the 'habit' of not liking yourself and being afraid to love yourself. You are a very good and sweet and loving being. You are a beloved daughter of God. Would you tell God that any of His children are unlikable or unlovable? You would not and could not because you know that this is not true.

"Spend some time each day contemplating what you can do every day, what tiny step you could take that day toward liking yourself and loving yourself. Eventually you will look forward to the opportunity to be honest, to the opportunity to put yourself out there. Eventually you may go to the one you are in relationship with now and say to him honestly, 'I am sorry I have not been truthful. I did not know that I was afraid that you might not like what you found and I did not know that I was afraid to love and be loved. I want to like who I am. I want to share that with you, and I want to learn to love and be loved.' You have everything you need to be able to make that statement and mean it.

"Know that the Holy Spirit is within you at all times. All you need do is go inside yourself and ask that you be aware of your connection with the Holy Spirit, and it will be done. Know that you can ask for anything and that all guidance and direction will be given to you. You are very loved indeed. Whether it frightens you or not, you are very loved indeed.

"Blessings to you, precious one. Amen."

Finding a Life Partner

Lisa: Dear Holy Spirit, I'm 35 years old and ready to open my heart to a true partner. I have honored myself in the past by leaving relationships that weren't right, yet I wonder if my idea of how I think it is supposed to be is preventing me from creating what I truly want. I don't want to settle.

I met a man recently and was very excited after our first date, but on our 2nd date, he seemed more excited about the possibility of sex than having a relationship. Do you have any insight that would give me more peace in this part of my life?

Holy Spirit: "Greetings and blessings to you precious one. Indeed, it is a joyous occasion to gather together with you in this way. Thank you for your letter and for your request.

"It is important to not have too many ideas about how a spiritual partnership should look. One cannot know what is best for them and can only open up to allowing the universe to partner them with the right person. There is not one particular person that is a soul mate to you. That is the bad news. The good news is that most of the men on the planet *could* be a soul mate to you when you truly become ready.

"To have the relationship that you want, it is as if you become ripe and ready to be plucked from being single, learning, growing, experiencing, and questioning. You become ripe for relationship. At the same moment that you become ripe, someone else on the planet will become ripe, and your paths will cross.

"There are many degrees of ripeness. You have crossed paths with some when you were unripe and so were they, and yet there was an attraction drawing you together. This was a process of learning and growing, so that you could become ripened and ready for plucking. You are still in that process and are very near to being ripe. It is now truly a matter of making a very deep decision. 'Now *is* the time, and *I am* open and ready to do this.' Then nothing will keep you from it. Then you have to get out of the way and allow the universe to set you up with the matching partner.

"It is one thing to have a list of requirements, and it is another thing to have faith in your Creator to match you up in full knowingness with the right partner for you, the one who will give you what it is you are truly seeking, which is growth, development, evolution, peace, love, happiness, distress, challenge, and everything that will give you your ultimate goal.

"Perhaps this person will not be in the package you have anticipated or may have issues that are very challenging. Perhaps that is the point, and perhaps not. Do not take the next person who steps into your life to be this life partner, but instead allow yourself to become fully ready, fully ripened. When the time comes and this person steps into your life, you will know it. You will not have doubts.

"There is much that you are open to, and there are fears as well. Your worst fears will happen whether you are with someone or not, if that is the state of your mind. It is important to become willing to risk your worst fears and then find the freedom on the other side. Examine your fears. Experience them. Try them on. Share them with others. Learn to laugh at them. Play the game of asking, 'What is the worst that can happen? And when that happens, what would be the worst that can happen?' Take it to the end and see that whatever happens is not the end of the world. It is just something that happens.

"There are many countless rewards in receiving a life partner. Countless does not begin to describe it, and yet becoming a life partner is even more rich. That is the process you are in now. Continue this unfolding of yourself, your heart, your mind, your fears, your dreams, and allow yourself to truly become ready, truly become open, and to know that all good things will be given to you as a result. You need not fear being alone forever, yet that is one of your fears to examine. Many gifts lay ahead of you, and it is important to be open to them so that you do not miss them on your journey.

"Blessings to you precious one. Amen.'"

An Empty Feeling within Me

Shannon: Dear Holy Spirit, I am a 27 year old wife and mother of two beautiful girls, ages two and four, yet, I still have this empty feeling within me. I have a lot to be thankful for and have a terrific family but still there is a void. I have gone through years of my life dealing with cancer in my family. My grandfather passed away almost 7 years ago from cancer, and my life just doesn't seem to be the same. My father then got prostate cancer only to be followed by a brain aneurism. Then my husband got testicular cancer to be followed by my grandmother with breast cancer. What do I do?

Holy Spirit: "Greetings and blessings to you precious one. Indeed, it is a joyous occasion to gather together with you in this way. Thank you for your letter and for your request.

"Indeed, you have had many challenges within your family. It is important to remember that these types of challenges are most often wake up calls. They are calls to those who are afflicted and to those who love them, to wake up in whatever ways one might be asleep. If any of those with cancer or any of those who love them have been seeking more faith, more awareness of God, a deeper, richer experience of God, a deeper appreciation for life, for nature, for family, for relationship, for those things that truly matter, often times a life threatening illness will do just that.

"If one has prayed for a richer experience of their life on earth, what better way than to be on the verge of losing it to appreciate it fully? You say there is a void within you, and perhaps this void is God. For you, despite how many life-threatening illnesses you are surrounded by, there is still a void where God is concerned. That in and of itself is a wake-up call. Each time there is something before you, such as an illness or a physical condition that threatens one's life, that is the time to stop what you are doing and join with God. That is the time to pray. That is the time to ask God to join you in your heart and mind and bring you comfort, bring you peace, bring you the knowing that regardless of what happens, everything is ok.

"You have so many opportunities and inspirations to join with God and now is the time to do that. Stop whatever you are doing, and join with God. Stop what you are doing and pray. Look around you and see what you have. It is so easy to focus on what you have lost and what you are losing and what you might lose, and now it is time to turn 180 degrees and become aware of what you have. Become aware of the richness and gifts and people and joy and beauty and grace in your life on a day to day basis. You have the laughter of your precious little daughters and the joy on their faces when you play with them. You have the witnessing of their learning and unfolding. You have the pleasure of a loving family. You have the beauty of all that is in front of you. There is so much richness, and yet the focus is on loss. You can see that what one focuses on becomes their reality.

"Perhaps the void is that you have turned your back on what is good and beautiful and wonderful and amazing in your world. It already exists. It is already there. You are just facing the other way. When you turn around you will see all of the beauty and the grace that you already have. It is so easy to turn away from the good in one's life when the focus is on tragedy. In what ways do you gain by focusing on tragedy? In what ways do you lose by turning away from the Life in your life?

"You have these two beautiful children brimming over with Life, and yet they cannot outweigh the tragic. Each of these experiences is your opportunity to join with God, to deepen your faith, to look around and see what you *do* have, to appreciate each moment, to appreciate waking up, to appreciate your family, to appreciate your home, to appreciate the ways that you laugh and learn and play and struggle and are challenged on a day to day basis, to deepen the gratitude you have for the wind and the rain and the sun and the snow and everything in between. It is a wake-up call. The ones in your life who have become sick have given you the gift of this opportunity of a wake-up call. Now it is time to wake up, the alarm is going off.

"Blessings to you, precious one. Amen."

Chapter Highlights

".... with the prospect of beginning a relationship, what you must do is expect and look forward to the opportunity to have your feelings hurt so that you can come to know yourself better, know the areas where you are challenged, and pray that those places become healed and whole and filled with faith and love rather than fear...."

"What is more realistic in making a lifetime commitment to someone is to make a commitment to who that person is in their entirety, to accept the things about them that you cannot change, and even different than that, to accept everything about them as potentially something that can never be changed...."

"The more you love you, the more you cannot do the things that do not serve you. The more you love you, the less room there is for anything other than that which is good. Spend more time loving you and there will be less room for these addictions. It is truly that simple."

"When you feel strong and confident in who you are, bring that into the world and allow another relationship to unfold in your life, being mindful not to lose yourself in the process. It is not to be self-centered when you step into a relationship, but to continue to make yourself, your relationship with God, your family, your work, your goals, and your priorities as important as they truly are."

"The real truth is that it is not safe to *not* love or be loved because if you do not love or are not loved, surely you will perish."

"One cannot know what is best for them and can only open up to allowing the universe to partner them with the right person. There is not one particular person that is a soul mate to you. That is the bad news. The good news is that most of the men on the planet *could* be a soul mate to you when you truly become ready."

————————

"If one has prayed for a richer experience of their life on earth, what better way than to be on the verge of losing it to appreciate it fully?"

14

Bringing God's Voice into the World

"When one can hear only God's Voice,
they can perceive only that Voice
in the one in front of them."

Holy Spirit: "When each perceived piece of God's Child is restored to Oneness and there is only One Child of God, then that Child will be restored to Its Father and returned safely Home. Each piece must be restored to the Oneness for the Oneness to be complete. As each perceived piece of God's Child remembers the Truth of who they are and brightens the flame of the Holy Spirit within them, they are then reminders to everyone they meet of the Truth of who they are. When you go out into the world with the Holy Spirit, you hear only the Holy Spirit in the one in front of you and you speak only the Words of the Holy Spirit. That is the pathway to the restoration of God's Child.

"Truth begets Truth. Love begets Love. And in every moment that you bring Truth and Love into the world, you create more Truth and Love in the world. And when that is all there is, the Oneness is complete. The world will have served its purpose, and God's Child will return to Its Father, resting peacefully in the knowledge of Its Perfection."

Candace's Story Continued

Candace: When I arrived in Silicon Valley to be with DavidPaul, it was the height of the Internet boom. I was not prepared for the pace of life and the different priorities and values there. Everyone I knew in Hawaii was on a spiritual path and wanted a deeper awareness and understanding of Truth; they knew about the work I did with the Holy Spirit and welcomed the opportunity to connect with this Voice through me. In Silicon Valley, the priority was stock options, and the few people who received sessions with the Holy Spirit would ask questions about their stock options.

Rarely sharing the Holy Spirit with others or listening on my own, I soon grew depressed and was guided to connect with the Holy Spirit each morning before beginning my day. I wrote down the communications I received and tried to apply them, but with so much going on in my life—leaving my Hawaiian paradise, losing my support system and friends, ending a three year relationship and beginning a new one—I wasn't very successful. Without being able to apply these messages, they were only helpful in the moments that I listened and remembered, which had become fewer and fewer as time went on.

Struggling with so much, my relationship with DavidPaul became strained. I began to lose my sense of purpose with this Voice, and before long, I was feeling very lonely and disheartened. In spite of these challenges, DavidPaul and I were determined to lead a guided life and do our best to do what was in our highest good, rather than what was easiest. Because of that, we checked in with the Holy Spirit every Sunday, which we called 'church,' and usually one time during the week as well. We asked questions about our relationship and sought guidance on seeing the best in one another. Through this connection with the Holy Spirit, we were able to work through these difficult times and eventually we became engaged.

For a while, life was wonderful. We spent much of our time planning our wedding and enjoying all that that entails, but after the honeymoon was over, our Silicon Valley life was back to normal. While we continued to check in with the Holy Spirit every week, we did it with the desire to receive answers, rather than with the intention to be connected with the Holy Spirit. For me, this took a lot of the meaning out of the relationship and didn't feed me the way I needed it to, although I didn't realize this at the time.

At some point, it seemed to me that life in Silicon Valley was not conducive to focusing on the Holy Spirit. This was not true, but it was what I came to believe while living there. As a result, I resigned myself to feeling less alive and less connected to the Holy Spirit. When our daughter, Hannah, was born a couple of years later, she was all I needed to nearly forget about the Holy Spirit altogether.

Hannah was a very high maintenance baby and demanded all the attention and energy I had to give, and I gave it to her. Two years quickly passed. Then I stopped nursing her and woke up one day with the remembrance that I wanted a more meaningful life. I adored my daughter and I loved being a mother, but I also needed more of a connection with God and the Holy Spirit, not to mention more of a connection with myself.

Around this time, DavidPaul and I were guided to write our family prayer, which would lead us in the direction of our true path. (See page 105 for our family prayer) Once we wrote our prayer, we were guided to say it over and over again throughout the day as if it were already true. As a result, I began to believe our prayer and my life began to unfold toward the intention of that prayer. I soon picked up ACIM again and also began to meditate. Before long, I was checking in more often and had reestablished my relationship with the Holy Spirit. I felt happier and more connected with Truth than I had in a long time.

Eventually, we were guided to move to Oregon. DavidPaul and I had had the same dream for as long as we could remember. We wanted to write a book that inspired and instructed people in how to hear the Holy Spirit. The Holy Spirit had told me since the beginning to walk my talk so that when this book was written, it would be as truthful and applicable as possible. In the process of moving, I realized that a window had opened up for us to write this book. The only problem was...I was still learning to walk my talk.

Like all relationships, my relationship with the Holy Spirit has had its ups and downs, though in this case, it was painfully clear that all of these ups and downs were my doing. Once we landed in Oregon, we enrolled our daughter in preschool part time and began to focus our energy and attention on meditation and the Holy Spirit. We spent our time connecting with God's Voice and seeking guidance for the book. In the course of receiving communication, I learned and remembered so much Truth that my concepts about DavidPaul, God, and the world began to change radically.

For so long, I thought that hearing the Holy Spirit was the goal, but in writing this book and in looking back on my struggles over the past ten years, I realize that hearing this Voice is only the first step. Beyond that, I need to learn how to use this Voice to guide my thoughts, my perceptions, my emotions, and therefore, my reality, so that I can live a happy life and move in the direction of Oneness with God and God's Child. I've come to see that having God's Voice is like having the right exercise machine. It's a great tool and it works, if I use it. If I don't, it just sits in the corner collecting dust or its function changes and it becomes something to hang things on.

Even though I can hear the Holy Spirit, I still have so much to learn about how to apply God's Voice to my life. My gift is sharing this Voice. My life lesson is learning how to use It—a lesson I have been resisting for many years. I am now slowly relearning how to experience that wonderful Presence in my mind Who makes loving observations wherever I go. I am realizing that there is only one True Voice in the world, and any others that I perceive, I made up. And I am remembering that the Holy Spirit is part of me and can guide me in all that I think and do in ways that can bring me unlimited peace.

I've often heard that people teach what they most need to learn, and this is certainly true for me. Recently, while reading ACIM, I read, "God's Voice asks of everyone one question only: Are you ready yet to help Me save the world?" I flashed back to my teenage years, to my 20's, to my social work degree, and to the work I've done. When people would ask me what I wanted to do with my life I would say, "I want to save the world!" Now I am learning what that really means. And it begins with a thought, not a step.

My goal is to one day hear only the Holy Spirit, and as the Holy Spirit said, that is not a matter of if, but when. The outcome is assured.

Hearing God's Voice in the World

DavidPaul: In the process of hearing God's Voice in the world, there have been times when Candace and I have questioned whether we were hearing the Voice of the Holy Spirit or hearing the voice of the ego. Holy Spirit, how can one truly know when they are hearing the Holy Spirit versus the ego?"

Holy Spirit: "There are, often times, many voices running around in one's head and more often than not, these are the voices of criticism, judgment, attack, or blame. They tell you what you did wrong, what you should have done differently, or how you could have done better. They tell you what that person did wrong, what they should not have done, and how they should have done it better. Those types of communications are the voice of the ego.

"You know you are hearing the Holy Spirit when what you hear is filled with Truth. It may not always be what you want to hear, so you may think, 'This Voice is telling me that this person in front of me who I have fallen in love with is not the person I will spend my life with.' You might feel angry at that Voice and you might think it is the ego because you do not like the answer, and yet, if you ask the Holy Spirit, 'Is this person in front of me the one I will spend my life with?' and if you hear an answer filled with Truth, whether it answers your question or not, or whether you like the answer or not, and there is no attack or blame or criticism or judgment, just Reality, you can know that you are hearing the Holy Spirit. Once you enter into judgment and attack and blame, you can know you are no longer hearing God's Voice.

"In particular, how you know you are hearing God's Voice is because you have asked to hear God's Voice. You have asked God or the Holy Spirit or Jesus to join with you and to communicate with you and give you guidance or direction or Truth. On one level or another, you have asked for that Voice. The ego, on the other hand, just rambles on and on within the mind without invitation because once you made the ego, the invitation was open. You cannot now un-invite the ego, but you *can* quiet the ego.

"In any moment that you notice that what you are hearing in your mind is not of Truth or of Love, you can stop for a moment and inquire within yourself as to what you are hearing, and if it is something that is judgmental or attacking, you can acknowledge that. If you want to, you can thank the ego for that input and then make a decision within yourself to hear Truth instead. You make the decision to no longer participate in that which is not real and you say, 'Holy Spirit, I would like to hear Truth.'

"It is similar to changing the radio station on your stereo. When a song comes on that you do not like, you click a button or turn the dial and you move on to the next song. You can do the same in your mind when you hear communication that you don't like or that is not serving you or feels painful. You can say instead, 'I want to hear God's Station,' and you click over to that one and you ask the Holy Spirit to communicate with you. It may be about something in particular or it may be a connection you are seeking. Words may come into your mind or it may be a feeling, a sense that the Holy Spirit is with you, God is with you, and in so doing, you quiet the ego and you turn up the volume on the Holy Spirit.

"The challenge of life in the world is how to notice when you are not listening to the Holy Spirit. Ultimately, there are only two voices to listen to: the ego or God's Voice. If the one you are listening to is painful, then you want to choose differently, and the challenge of life in the world is to notice when what you are listening to is painful. It has become such a habit, such a way of life to take in and absorb and believe and think about and act on all that comes to us in our mind from the ego, when none of it is true, none of it exists, and none of it serves us.

"In noticing when your thinking is painful, and that can be anything from thinking 'This water is probably contaminated,' when you pour yourself a glass of water to 'I am late. I never have enough time. I can't get everything done,' to 'I wonder why my father hasn't called. He should have called by now. Maybe he doesn't want to talk to me.' Those simple, seemingly benign thoughts that you encounter millions of times throughout one day are thoughts that cause you pain without even realizing it. Instead you can choose to think with the Holy Spirit so that you can have peace and faith in those moments rather than pain.

"It is the choosing that, in fact, is the most difficult. Hearing God is your most natural ability. It is your natural right and natural gift and that which has never been gone from you except with your thinking. But choosing to hear that Voice, choosing to quiet the ego, choosing to turn up the volume on the Holy Spirit, that can be challenging indeed. In order to do that, you must become aware of your thinking. You must become aware of your thoughts and how they are serving you or not serving you and how to replace the ones that are not serving you with thoughts of Truth and Peace.

"When you have thoughts that are serving you, acknowledge them, give thanks for them, take a moment to appreciate them, and continue to seek more. The more that you practice changing stations, the easier it will be to stay tuned to the frequency that truly serves you. Ultimately, there will come a day when your radio tuner is programmed only to the station of the Holy Spirit and it does not leave that station any more. Eventually all you will hear is God's Voice, Right-Thinking, Truth and Reality in any given situation, which would then mean you have been restored to your natural state.

"One thinks that this goal is monumental, impossible, daunting, and yet all it means is that you are being restored to your natural state, that of only hearing the Voice of your Father, only hearing Truth, only seeing Truth as a result. You no longer hear or see the world, as was Jesus's experience, and the peace and the comfort and the love that come from only hearing that Voice, no matter what seems to be happening in the world, is so invaluable because all there is is Love and Peace and Truth. And there is no opposite. There is no up and down, back and forth, left and right. There is only Love and Peace and Truth. There is nothing to compare it to or contrast it with, but only to rejoice in that restored state.

"When Jesus appeared to walk upon the earth, his goal was to only hear God's Voice. His goal was to no longer hear the ego or participate in any of the ideas of the ego but rather hear Truth, follow Truth, and share Truth. Over the course of that lifetime, Jesus accomplished that goal and only heard Truth. Being in a body and having experienced the ego, Jesus was able to understand the thoughts in the minds of the ones in front of him, while at the same time knowing that none of the thoughts of the world were true.

"When one came to him and talked about their life, their situation in the world, sickness, death, and so on, Jesus heard them and knew from where they were speaking and yet did not believe in what they were saying and did not join them in those thoughts. He had so much certainty that what they were saying was not true, whether they were sick or maimed or dying or dead, because he could only hear Truth. He could touch them and talk to them with so much certainty and so much confidence and Truth that their illness, their injury, or their dying would fall away because in fact it was not true. It was not that he was a miracle worker so much as that he did not believe the illusions of the world and could not participate in them. He could not see illness or injury. He could not see dying or death as it is known in the world, and when one saw through his eyes, it all fell away.

"It seems to those in the world that the task of hearing only the Holy Spirit is so enormous and so daunting that it could not be possible and yet that is the whole purpose of Jesus's life—to show you that, in fact, it is possible. Jesus was not special in the sense of being more capable or being more loved by God to be able to hear only the Holy Spirit. Jesus just dedicated every moment of his life on the earth to that end and, of course, it came about. That is the only difference. Different goals, different dreams, different desires, and different outcomes. You are not different from Jesus in your ability to pursue the same goal or in your ability to carry out the same dream and the same intention.

"Jesus fabricated a most horrific death by the world's standards to show that even while the worst was happening, it did not matter. It was not real. Jesus did not perceive that death. Jesus only perceived that which was Real. Jesus only perceived God's Son, God, and the Holy Spirit, which has absolutely nothing to do with the world, anything in the world, bodies, death, crucifixions, or anything else. Jesus loved equally the ones who seemed to appear in front of him, be they his mother or brother or persecutors because he understood that they were Him…. They were God's Son.

"When one can hear only God's Voice, they can perceive only that Voice in the one in front of them. Because God's Voice is in everyone, it is so easy to perceive Truth in the one in front of you. It is so easy to perceive God in the one in front of you when you can perceive that in yourself. When that is all you see in you, that will be all you see in your brother; it would not be possible to see anything else.

"Becoming very clear about what it is you truly want and then dedicating every moment to that with just your thinking, nothing else but your thinking, you too can have that which you seek. One thinks that to dedicate every moment to their purpose means being on their knees in a monastery somewhere or to be of service like Mother Teresa. What it means is that in every moment you are aware of what you are thinking and you choose the kind of thinking that serves you and the world in such a way that only that which you truly desire can unfold. Know that God's Voice is with you every thought of the way, is there for the choosing, and has as Its only desire, to serve you."

Exercise—Observing Your Thoughts

Holy Spirit: "Set aside a quiet time, turn off the phone, put a note on the door, get comfortable, and close your eyes. You can pray. You can meditate. Spend as many minutes as you would like doing either or both. Connect with God. Connect with yourself. Connect with the Holy Spirit. Make a statement for yourself that you would like to hear God's Voice, and imagine that as you make that declaration, the Holy Spirit accepts your invitation and joins with you. It has no other function but to do so.

"You can either begin a dialogue with the Holy Spirit and listen for the answer, or you can sit and notice the thoughts that come into your mind. The thoughts that are loving and kind and truthful come from your Right-Mind, from the Holy Spirit, while the ones that are not are the thoughts of the ego. And as you notice the thoughts that are of the ego, do not worry about them, be frightened by them, or be angry with them, just note, 'right now, I am thinking with the ego mind,' and put your attention back on God-Mind and allow your thoughts again to resume from God-Mind. Allow yourself to engage in this practice of just noticing the thoughts, allowing yourself to recognize where they come from, not judging them or fearing them, just noticing them, and continuing to refocus on the thoughts of the Holy Spirit.

"You may become distracted at some point and off on some adventure somewhere in your thinking; when you notice this, just bring yourself back. There is nothing to be disappointed in or mad at. Just bring yourself back to here and now, with the thought and desire and intention to connect with Right-Mindedness. Interact with your thoughts in this way for as long as you can, and when you are complete, you can give thanks to the Holy Spirit for the Right-Mindedness that you have available to you at all times. It is there for your choosing and is there only to serve you, and nothing you can think or do could ever change that."

Using God's Voice in the World

DavidPaul: Connecting with Truth and hearing this Voice can happen anywhere, anytime. It does not matter if you're in an important meeting, on the subway, riding a bike, sitting in traffic, working out, or waiting tables. It is possible to connect with Truth and hear the Voice for Truth in all that we do in life. This is why hearing God's Voice does not mean that we have to change our lives, become different people, or give up that which we love. It simply means to connect with God in our daily lives, to see the world through His eyes, and to hear His loving Words so that we may be filled with peace, acceptance, and understanding. In so doing, we bring the Holy Spirit and Heaven into the world, into our families, into our companies, and into everything we do.

We each have our own purpose for hearing and using this Voice in our lives. Discovering this purpose may be simple for some or a challenging process for others. In either case, coming to understand and accept how and why we hear and use this Voice can be an incredible gift.

Living with Candace, I have compared my hearing of the Holy Spirit to hers dozens of times over the years. To me, she seems to hear the Voice in a slightly different way than I do, in a way that allows her to share this Voice with other people more naturally.

Candace has been sharing this Voice since the first week she ever heard It. I, on the other hand, have never shared this Voice with anyone else except Candace. Even though I check in with the Holy Spirit on my own all the time and receive wonderful communication, I humbly admit that sharing this Voice in the way that she does frightens me. Hearing the Holy Spirit for myself is very doable and rewarding, but the fear of mucking up the words for someone else or not doing the Voice of the Holy Spirit justice is just too great. While I sometimes stumble when I'm checking in by myself, I know it's no big deal. I just say it over again. Or if something doesn't quite sound right or doesn't come out perfectly, I instinctually know what was meant or I take a moment, reconnect, and do it again. But the fear of doing that in front of someone else, or worse, a group of people, is too enormous. I always thought that I would get over this before we wrote our first book together, but I haven't.

One morning while we were checking in with the Holy Spirit, I felt very disappointed for not providing as many communications from the Holy Spirit for the book as Candace had. For the most part, it just seemed easier and better to have her check in on the questions. She's used to doing it. She's good at it. And I just thought she could do a better job than me. At the same time, I really wanted to show people that anyone could do it. I don't consider hearing the Holy Spirit a "gift" of mine. It's something I've opened up to with practice and determination…. So if I can do it, anyone can.

As I sat there feeling disappointed, I asked the Holy Spirit for communication.

Holy Spirit: "Everyone has a different function and a different job. Everyone chose their job and their function, and being the introvert that you are, you have a very strong need to have your own sense of personal peace on a moment-to-moment, hour-to-hour, day-to-day basis. When you look at Candace, you see that her discipline and her struggles and challenges do not involve choosing peace on a consistent basis—certainly sometimes, and certainly eventually—but the desire for peace is not there at the moment of awareness of pain.

"What you signed up for with the Holy Spirit was to have your own personal, real, obvious, and blatant connection so that you would have this resource for peace within you. That is the service you signed up for with the Holy Spirit. Do not think that Candace's is a 'higher service' or anything like that because she can share these Words with other people in this way. When you use the Holy Spirit for Its true intention, for Its true function, to serve you in experiencing peace, to shift your perspectives to Truth, and to remember your Oneness with God, that's it. Then you live that and you become a walking demonstration of that. That's what you signed up for. You have watched this one and witnessed what she has signed up for and that is not what you were interested in, is that true?"

DavidPaul: In what ways? I wouldn't mind sharing the Holy Spirit with people.

Holy Spirit: "Even if you did not choose having your own peace?"

DavidPaul: No. I would rather have my peace than be able to share the Holy Spirit.

Holy Spirit: "And coincidentally, that's what you have. You got exactly what you wanted and what you signed up for. Candace, being an extrovert, a talker, social, more external, signed up for this, does a good job at it, and does not always choose peace at the awareness of pain. It's not to say that one is right or wrong, but it's also not to say that one is a higher calling or anything like that. They are just different. By the nature of each personality, they serve God differently. Truly, by the nature of your essence, you have a certain path you go on.

"You have a wonderful gift of the desire to seek and to choose peace and to use the Holy Spirit in that way. It is important for you to talk about this in the book...that Candace has the ability to share communication with other people while your strength currently lies in experiencing your own peace in times of trouble, your Oneness with God when you are feeling separated.

"There are so many different ways for people to use the Holy Spirit or to fulfill their function with the Holy Spirit. Yours is more intimate and more personal. Candace's is more outward, and she offers that to everyone. It is not to try to imitate what Candace is demonstrating but to find your own groove, your own rhythm, and your own connection in relationship with the Holy Spirit.

"What you have can only be what you have chosen, and there is a part of you that is very aware that this is exactly as you would like it to be. You have a very strong desire to be of service and you have the belief that this is a way of being of service that you feel would work for you. You could say, 'I share the Voice of God with people and that is my service,' and yet, you have to contemplate what service really is. Is it what one lives and how they think, how they use their mind, or is it what one says out loud? So reshape or reframe for yourself what kind of service you would like to do, in Truth. Would you rather have your peace in this moment or share the Words of the Holy Spirit with someone else? It is very obvious to you what you would choose. This is not to say you can only have one. That is not the point. The point is that *in this moment*, that is what you are choosing.

"You have a desire to use the Holy Spirit in the way that your mate does because you have witnessed that sharing, have gained so much from it, and have seen others gain from it. You desire to have that too, and yet it is not your function. That can be disappointing or frustrating at times, and yet you would not compromise what you have with the Holy Spirit for anything. You desire to use the Holy Spirit to gain peace and insight and a shift in perspective more than being of service, with your beliefs of what being of service is. As you utilize the Holy Spirit in this way more and more, live the Truths that you hear, and seek peace more frequently, you are living in the world in such a way that that *is* your service. Just holding the belief and the Reality of the Holy Spirit and what the Holy Spirit can offer you *is* your service. Whether or not you share those Words with others has nothing to do with it.

"Candace experiences peace in sharing the Words, and there can be more benefit for her in sharing the Words with others and hearing the Message that way than in seeking peace directly and getting an answer just for her. She often gets her answers through receiving answers for other people.

"Others may fulfill their function and utilize their relationship with the Holy Spirit in the way that they create a marriage, a family, a business, an organization that supports children or women in Afghanistan, or someone who writes music or songs of Truth or poetry or something like that. So many people are manifesting their relationship with the Holy Spirit on earth whether it's conscious or not. Often times, they just don't discuss that part of their lives with others."

Recognizing God's Voice in the World

Candace: Holy Spirit, what happens when one begins to recognize the Holy Spirit in the world?

Holy Spirit: "As one engages with the Holy Spirit more and more, through prayer, meditation, walking in the world engaged in conversation with the Holy Spirit, seeking guidance, direction, comfort, and union, this begins to build on itself and a trust is gained in the relationship because it is unlike any other relationship one has experienced in the world.

"It is difficult to conceive of and believe that, in fact, the Holy Spirit is part of you and cannot be separated from you. The Holy Spirit holds the deepest experience of Truth you are capable of having. As one walks around in the world, having come to believe that the Holy Spirit is their true Self, true Companion, true Guide, true Love, they will shine in that awareness. It will be this huge blushing that is so bright as to be overwhelming at times, and as a result, one will look upon another, whomever that may be in the world, and not be able to help but recognize the Holy Spirit in the one across from them, the one behind them, the one to the left of them, and so on. It will be impossible to look out in the world at another and not see the Holy Spirit in front of you. Everywhere you look will be the Holy Spirit and this is what you will acknowledge and recognize and validate in the one in front of you because you cannot help it and that is what will come alive in them as a result. Everywhere you go, you will touch that part of them that you share with them because, in fact, you are One with everyone who appears to be separate on the earth. You will come to understand and believe in the Oneness, and your only desire will be to acknowledge the Holy Spirit in everyone you encounter because in so doing, the Oneness becomes stronger, more real, more aware, and a momentum builds that will eventually take over, and that is a ride you cannot wait to get on.

"So little is asked of you while you venture off in this dream, but whatever is asked is only done so that you can fully remember and experience the Truth and the Joy of who and what you really are, and the Holy Spirit is waiting patiently, patiently, patiently within you to join you on that ride."

Chapter Highlights

"It is so easy to perceive God in the one in front of you when you can perceive that in yourself. When that is all you see in you, that will be all you see in your brother; it would not be possible to see anything else."

"As one walks around in the world, having come to believe that the Holy Spirit is their true Self, true Companion, true Guide, true Love, they will shine in that awareness. It will be this huge blushing that is so bright as to be overwhelming at times, and as a result…it will be impossible to look out in the world at another and not see the Holy Spirit in front of you."

15

Being God's Voice in the World

"The Light of God in me
rekindles the Light in all of God's children."

Holy Spirit: "Hearing God's Voice is more than hearing Words being spoken to you. It is the opportunity to live a life where your purpose is understood. Hearing God's Voice is the opportunity to bring meaning to your life and understanding to your experiences. God's Voice can be for you a way of life, a way to live in the world with Truth rather than beautiful Words you hear on occasion. Though the Words may be lovely, it is what you do with Them that matters."

Remembering the Truth of Who You Are

DavidPaul: Holy Spirit, what is the purpose of life on earth?
Holy Spirit: "Most people walk around in the world feeling at least a little bit unfulfilled, unsatisfied, and wondering what their purpose is or what is the meaning of life. The meaning of life is to give you the opportunity to remember the Truth of who you really are, and your purpose is the same, though by remembering that, you then remind another. That is your true purpose.

"It seems that each of God's children in the world has at least some awareness that something is missing, that somehow they are not complete. They look for completion in a partner, a child, a job, a thing, and yet even with all of that, there is still a sense that something is missing. This something is their connection to the One Child of God and their relationship with their Father.

"When one perceives themselves as separate and perceives another as the enemy, it is impossible to remember that they are, along with the one in the front of them, along with that 'enemy,' God's Child. God's Child is not complete without all of the perceived 'enemies' upon the earth, and this is a painful existence when one is not able to remember the Truth of themselves as well as the one in front of them.

"If each one is seeking the remembering of their Oneness with each other and their relationship to God, this is not something that can happen in an instant and then be let go. It is something that must become a way of life, something that must be lived out every day, ultimately in every moment, so that you have the satisfaction and the fulfillment and the Oneness that you are.

"When one begins to remember who they really are and begins to see that Truth in the one in front of them, their whole perspective of the world and its purpose changes. The Holy Spirit is there for you in every moment, at every turn, at every stop and start; and the Holy Spirit's desire is to join with you, guide you, direct you, and translate for you so that you may be on your true path Home."

Living the Truth of Who You Are

DavidPaul: Holy Spirit, how can one come to live the Truth of who they are?

Holy Spirit: "The ability to hear God's Voice is a wonderful gift, and it is your natural right. The ability to choose this Voice is a very powerful and peaceful experience as well. The ability to truly listen to what you hear after choosing and then take what you have heard and apply it to your life, apply it to yourself, and apply it to the one in front of you is what gives meaning to your existence. This is not done in a moment here or a moment there, but rather ideally, it becomes a way of life, a practice that you follow that serves you throughout your life. This is what one could call their true religion.

"You determine for yourself what it is that you truly want and then you envision what a life with that priority would look like and how that might unfold. From there, you begin to create a practice of that lifestyle so that the memory, the choosing, the hearing, the listening, and the applying become a regular practice of yours so that you may have or bring peace wherever you go.

"One's true religion is understanding what they value, what they seek, how to go about that, and how to live it out. It is a way of knowing how to be in any moment. You don't have to wonder, 'What is right? What should I do? Where do I go?' In any situation, you can instead practice your religion, whatever that is for you. You will be guided and led toward Truth and there will not be room for doubt or despair. When one has their own true religion, which is just to say their own True relationship with God that is lived out in the world, there is the consistent remembering of who they really are, which begins to become more of a belief than a theory.

"The more that you remember the Truth of who you are, the more you will experience yourself as that. The more that you hear the Holy Spirit and choose to hear the Holy Spirit, the more you will hear the Holy Spirit and the more you will be able to choose the Holy Spirit.

"Eventually, you will only hear one Voice and that will be the worldly pinnacle of your true religion. You will have this Voice within you at all times, not just when you choose, but at all times, to know how to be in the world in a way that brings meaning and purpose to you.

"The gift of the Holy Spirit has already been given to you. The ability to hear this Voice has already been given to you. In Truth, there is no choice to make. Only one Voice really exists, and the ability to think and hear and speak with that Voice is already accomplished. Now it is just a matter of finding that place deep within you where you know It is True, settling into that Truth, and living It out."

DavidPaul's Story Continued

DavidPaul: Looking back, being in relationship with Candace has been both my greatest gift and my greatest challenge. The first week Candace arrived from Hawaii to be with me, we went to Magic Mountain, an amusement park in Southern California, to celebrate. Although we had never exchanged a single kiss before her arrival, we loved each other deeply and were feeling incredibly alive and joyful at the thought of starting a life and a family together.

While eating lunch on the grass that day at Magic Mountain, we closed our eyes for a few minutes and joined with the Holy Spirit. The Holy Spirit spoke to us about the magic of our union, why we were together, and the incredible gifts and rewards awaiting us in our future. But before we opened our eyes, the Holy Spirit said one thing that remains etched in my mind—the Holy Spirit told us that our union with one another would be quite a roller coaster ride, that we would have breathtaking highs and heart-wrenching lows and both would be a part of the ride.

Afterward, we held hands and looked into each other's eyes. Filled with excitement and hope for our future together, we talked about the challenges the Holy Spirit forewarned us about and made a commitment to see one another through God's Eyes in times of struggle and pain. I thought that my love for Candace was so strong and my understanding of Truth so unshakable that choosing Right-Mindedness would be an easy commitment to make.

Seven years have passed since that day at Magic Mountain. While I love Candace with all my heart and am so grateful for our life together, I humbly admit that our union has been the scariest, most challenging ride of my life. I have zoomed higher than I ever dreamed I would, but I have also plunged lower than I ever imagined I could—over and over and over again. I thought that my desire for peace, my understanding of Truth, and my know-how for choosing was enough, but I have continued to find myself saying and doing things I don't enjoy or prefer.

As Candace and I sat down to write this chapter with the Holy Spirit, I have to admit that I struggled to understand how knowing and living one's true religion applied to me. Then one day, Candace and I got into a fight. In the thick of it, I said some things that I wished I hadn't. When I stormed back to my office to calm down, a wave of melancholy came over me. I felt incredibly hopeless and sad for being so reactive and for not dealing with my thoughts and emotions more constructively, yet again. As I slumped on the couch in defeat, I closed my eyes and joined with the Holy Spirit.

"What could I possibly do to stop myself from acting this way?" I asked despairingly.

To my surprise, after more than an hour of talking with the Holy Spirit, the answer I walked away with was "living my true religion." What unfolded during that hour was a dialogue that taught me the power of using a single, repeatable process for choosing peace in any situation. What I currently had was a hodge-podge of perspectives, goals, and techniques that I had collected over the past ten years and used haphazardly. Through my conversation with the Holy Spirit, I came to understand how knowing my true religion and developing a simplified approach to living it could support me in manifesting my heart's desire. This was an incredible revelation for me.

The following week, I sat down with the Holy Spirit to learn how to put my true religion into practice.

Holy Spirit: "Indeed, we have been waiting for this day, patiently and lovingly, knowing that this would truly be a moment of bringing this Voice into the world in such a way as to inspire you to truly *live* with this Voice. Thank you for wanting to more fully live the Truth of who you are in the world so that you know in every moment that what you are thinking and saying and doing is indeed that which is in your highest good. To know this in every moment is to experience your union with God. That is ultimately what you are seeking in your life and in your desire to determine how to live your true religion.

"For you, your true religion is peace. It is what you came here to deepen. It is what you entered the world to more fully experience, and it is what you have come here to share with others. For you, peace is knowing the Truth of who you are, experiencing that Truth in your heart and mind, and sharing that Truth with all who truly want that for themselves, sharing that Truth with all who ask for it and who are open and willing to receive it—that is your true definition of peace, the definition you seek in your heart and mind to experience and live out in the world. So how then shall we experience this more fully together in your wakeful life?"

DavidPaul: The Holy Spirit and I then spent the better part of an hour discussing what this might look like. We also defined a simple process to help me experience peace more consistently, one that I could apply in any situation. While I was told that this process would continue to unfold over time, I am now using it in my daily life. While I don't expect my life to change overnight, nor do I believe I will always choose peace instead of pain from here on out, I feel very hopeful and excited to be applying it to my life, and I look forward to seeing where living my true religion takes me....

Exercise—Discovering Your True Religion

Holy Spirit: "Sit with a pencil and paper and write down all of the things that matter the most to you. This might be a way of feeling, a way of being, a way of doing, a way of seeing, rather than a favorite television show or your pet. Write down that which is most important to you that gives you satisfaction and fulfillment and brings you joy or peace or comfort. This might be something like loyalty, honesty, caring, acceptance…. These types of things.

"Then think for yourself, 'What are my ultimate goals? What are my higher goals in how I want to live?' Do you want to love your neighbor, extend kindness wherever you go? Do you want to turn the other cheek? Do you want to see God in everyone you meet? Do you want to hear God's Voice? Do you want to be restored to your Oneness? Whatever it may be, think about what your ultimate goals are. List them and prioritize them so that you can discover for you, truly, what is most important.

"With that information, begin to contemplate how you could live that would incorporate all that matters to you. Spend some time in prayer with this list. Share your list with God. Spend some time in meditation with this list. Share it with the Holy Spirit. Ask for whatever guidance or direction can be given to you that you may come to understand how it is that you would like to live. Allow this guidance and direction to come in any form it may. You might perceive an answer while driving down the road, when you wake from a dream, or after an encounter with another person. You may hear communication. You may get an insight or an inspiration. However it comes, begin to gather the pieces of guidance and direction that come to you. This may take days or weeks or longer.

"As you gather together all of these pieces, you may want to make notes about the guidance and direction you receive and begin to establish for yourself a framework for how you want to live in the world so that your life unfolds in the ways that bring you peace or joy or comfort and that leads you in the direction of your highest goals. You might ask yourself in a challenging situation, 'What would I do or how would I act if I were the person that I want to be?' You will get an answer in one form or another about what to say or do or think that supports you in that which matters the most to you. And when you stop and ask yourself, 'How is it that I can be who I dream of being?' and you receive some insight or direction and you follow through with that, then you *are* doing and being that which is your highest goal. It is not something that is out in the future, seemingly unattainable, too lofty to even imagine. It is something that you are doing and being right now because you have determined what it is, how to get there, and are questioning yourself as you go along to keep you in line with your goal.

"If you want to be a certain person one day, why not this day? Now that you know what that is and how to get there, it is very simple. This is what one could call their true religion. It is what they believe in, what matters to them, who they want to be, how they want to live in the world, how they want to interact with another, how they want to perceive.... It is *their* true religion, which has nothing to do with anyone else. It is only between you and God and the Holy Spirit, and it affords you a way of living and perceiving that enriches you in all the ways that matter to you."

Chapter Highlights

"When one begins to remember who they really are and begins to see that Truth in the one in front of them, their whole perspective of the world and its purpose changes."

―――――――

"When one has their own true religion, which is just to say their own true relationship with God that is lived out in the world, there is the consistent remembering of who they really are, which begins to become more of a belief than a theory."

A Note from the Authors

Writing this book has been our dream, the dream of sharing Who and What the Holy Spirit truly is, It's function and purpose in the world, and how we can use this Voice to guide our way Home. It is our hope that this book will empower you with everything you need to have a rich and rewarding relationship with God and the Holy Spirit all the rest of your days.

We also dream of working with people one-on-one, in workshops and retreats, over the phone, online, and wherever and however we can to help bring this Voice to life within them in real and undeniable ways. We look forward to the day when countless people all over the world are hearing and choosing this Voice. Whether you already hear this Voice or are opening up to It, we look forward to joining you in making this dream a Reality.

Blessings to you,

DavidPaul and Candace Doyle

Questions & Answers

"We can only fear what we don't understand.
Know that eventually all will be understood,
so there is no need to fear in the meantime."

Holy Spirit: "While any answer given to any question asked can have a different meaning for each person listening, an answer that is filled with Truth can be a reminder of Truth within God's Child. When one hears God's Words, it is as if an alarm goes off inside of them, reminding them that they are more than they seem to be in this moment. Any answer can be a reminder of Truth if perceived in such a way, and yet, Truth itself can penetrate illusions and stir you in your sleep."

Feeling Disconnected from God

DavidPaul: In thinking that God is not involved in my life or that God doesn't know what's going on with me in the world, I sometimes feel more disconnected from God and only further away from Him. Holy Spirit, do you have any communication for me on this?

Holy Spirit: "The thought that God did not create the world and God does not come into the world or exist within the world can be frightening or threatening for many, and yet that is the good news. God did not create the world, nor is God in it. It was made from your own thought and from your own thinking and continues to unfold and evolve as a result of your thinking. If you want to have God in the world, then *be* God in the world. Your ancestral line allows you to be God in the world. By recognizing the Truth of who you are, by recognizing the

197

Truth of the one in front of you, you bring God into the world with your think-ing and with your experience of the Truth of yourself and another.

"It is easy to think that you have been abandoned by God or that God isn't here for you in the world, when the Reality is, *you* are not here. You are not *in* the world. The world is just a thought. In Reality, you are just playing with God, happy, contented, and at peace while you seem to be having this dream. Just as God does not enter the world, in Truth, neither do you because it does not exist.

"While you perceive yourself here in the world, you can be connected with God in any and every moment that you desire. If the world does not exist, you need not fight your way out of it to be with God. Settle into your heart and mind for a moment and into the Reality that you have never been separate from God. Take a moment to acknowledge that, to connect with God, to experience the Truth of that, and remember or recognize that this is just a dream. In each moment that you do that, you transcend the world and you are joined with God.

"God is joined with you eternally—nonstop. So when *you* recognize that *you* are joined with God, then you give yourself that experience as well. Each time you perceive what you think might be of God in the world—whether it is a star, a person, a painting, or a ripe berry—you can stop and connect with God and the Truth of what really is, enjoying your dream as it appears and allowing it to serve you in connecting with God while you seem to live in the world."

Sermon on the Mount

DavidPaul: Holy Spirit, if Jesus was only hearing and speaking the Words of the Holy Spirit when he delivered the Sermon on the Mount, why do his mes-sages in the Bible seem so different than those in this book?

Holy Spirit: "The Bible is a storybook. People have written down historical stories that are either made up or have happened and have been passed down, and as the stories have been passed, they were written down to the best of one's ability to remember what they were told. Over time, the stories have changed and evolved. Certain things are more imagined than factual because of the way that the memory seems to work, and other things have been altered due to agendas. You can't believe everything you read.

"Many of the quotes found in the Bible that are attributed to Jesus are consid-erably accurate, but not all. In addition, the experience of communicating to a group of people two thousand years ago and in a part of the world in a time and place that had its own troubles, Jesus spoke to people where they were, which could reflect the place and the time. There was a profound belief in heaven and hell, good and evil, and these types of things and it would be difficult to not make reference to them.

"There are many today who have a strong belief in heaven and hell and good and evil, yet it is clear to so many that these concepts are not True. You can go through anything, including the Bible, line by line and ask what it means to you. What is it that you want to get out of this message? What is it that you want to gain from hearing this? What can you learn as a result?

"These messages are passed down for that reason only, not to become dogma, rules, and imprisoning beliefs, but to be for each one who reads them, a message of Truth. And with a Truth-filled message, it is possible to continue to glean insight and revelation from the same message over and over again in a variety of different ways. The same words will take on new meanings and meet different needs and fulfill different purposes than when you originally read them.

"If you feel in your heart that a message from the Bible that is attributed to Jesus is not True, disregard it. There are people who believe that whatever the Bible says is literally God's Word and that every word must be heeded. The Bible is a storybook filled with stories that offer messages to you that you can take if they serve you and leave if they don't.

"If you read the Sermon on the Mount and you gain certain insights, perspectives, or truths that nurture you and support you and are meaningful to you, then enjoy them; and if not, let them go. There is no need to throw out the whole book because there are some small parts that anger, confuse, or disillusion you, but rather take what serves you and leave the rest."

Heaven and Hell

Candace: Holy Spirit, what is heaven and hell?

Holy Spirit: "Heaven and hell are both belief systems. They are not actual places that exist. Hell is a state of mind rather than a place deep in the earth run by the devil, who also does not exist. Hell and the devil are merely one's thinking, one's mind that is unexamined and misinterpreted. Heaven is just the opposite. It is a state of mind that is examined and interpreted through Truth.

"There is a very little difference between heaven and hell. One can be in hell one moment and in heaven the next, and vice versa. They exist side by side in one's thinking. Ultimately, it is only a matter of believing or not believing what you think as to whether you are in hell or not.

"Heaven is a place of Right-Mindedness or perceiving with Truth. Ultimately, heaven is peace. When one has no beliefs that are troubling them and no thoughts that are calling for their attention, when one is thinking with Right-Mindedness and perceiving with Truth, one is in a state of heaven. No struggle, no pain—just peace. If the world does not exist, neither do heaven and hell as a physical location, only as a state of mind. They are both easily attainable...but choosing is up to you."

Angels and Spirit Guides

Candace: Holy Spirit, where do angels and spirit guides fit into all of this?

Holy Spirit: "Because the world is a long dream, it is possible to make any-thing within it, and you will make in your own reality whatever it is that can assist you or guide you in moving along in the direction that you seek. If you have the belief that a spirit guide could help you, then you will invent a spirit guide to help you. If you have the belief that the angels are here to serve you, then you will invent angels to serve you, and yet they are as illusory as your body, and all that you see in the world, and your brother as separate from you. However, whatever one invents to assist them in the ways they desire is fine; and those angels, spirit guides, and so on serve this purpose. They have all of the meaning that you give them and they provide the service that you decide. It can be a way of you hearing yourself, hearing God's Voice, or hearing Truth in a capacity that you welcome. And in that way, they serve you, though they are invented in your mind."

Hearing God's Voice in Others

Candace: Holy Spirit, how do you serve as a Translator between people?

Holy Spirit: "Most think upon the Holy Spirit as the Translator for God in the sense of God being this big booming Presence in Heaven whose Voice is pro-jected into the world and the Holy Spirit translates, and yet because everyone is a Child of God and has the Holy Spirit within them, the Holy Spirit can be used as a Translator for the one in front of you as well as for God. If you are having a conversation with someone, the Holy Spirit can translate for you what they are saying so that you hear their words as the language of Love, the language of Right-Mindedness, the language of God. You do not hear what appears to be coming from their physical body regarding the world. You hear, instead, the Holy Spirit.

"You can hear the Holy Spirit within your own mind translating God and God's Words to you so that you can speak God's Words into the world and can share these Words with the one in front of you, and at the same time, you can hear God's Words in front of you with that Translator in your Right-Mind. It is the same Holy Spirit that is in the one in the front of you and all the other ones upon the earth, so it is the Holy Spirit in the one in the front of you or within you that allows the words to be translated, either as they leave their lips or as they reach your ears.

"The gift of this Translation is heavenly indeed, and it is just like learning any new language. At first, it is difficult to understand. You may not understand any of it. Then you are able to pick out words and pieces. Over time, you are able to understand much of what is being said, and eventually you are able to speak that language to another. The words begin to come more freely and be more understood and well received, and the more you practice that language and live with that language, the more it becomes your own. Soon, there comes a time when it is so natural to speak in that language that you do not have to think first and you find yourself speaking it to one who does not know it, because it has become such a natural expression.

"Whether you have a knack for languages or not, this one is your true first language. Once you begin to hear it and understand it, it will come back to you, and it will be easier and more natural to you than whatever language you have been speaking in the world. The Holy Spirit is your first true language."

Winning the Lottery

DavidPaul: Holy Spirit, how can the Holy Spirit be used to be successful in the world, on Wall Street, win the lottery, become famous, etc?

Holy Spirit: "One might have the idea that to have God's Voice within them means to have a Resource for worldly gain. The Holy Spirit's only function is to restore your mind to Right-Thinking. It is not possible for the Holy Spirit to benefit you on Wall Street, win the lottery, or any other worldly function. It is literally not an ability that the Holy Spirit has because none of that exists, and it has nothing to do with Right-Mindedness.

"If you were to ask the Holy Spirit about winning the lottery, you may get a set of lottery numbers. They may win or they may not. The Holy Spirit's function is to guide you and assist you in your thinking to understand that all of that is just an illusion and that where you seek to fill the void with riches, you are truly looking for the Richness of God. You truly seek God's Love to fill that void, and no amount of lottery winnings will ever do that.

"You will always receive the Truth from the Holy Spirit. You may receive guidance, and yet it may or may not mean that you buy or sell at the right time. What causes one to buy or sell at the time are their belief systems, their own fear, and their own understanding of the world. One may receive guidance, and yet if the Holy Spirit were to give the same guidance to ten different people, it would be perceived and experienced ten different ways based upon one's thinking and one's ability to perceive the communication in any given moment. You will receive the guidance and then do with it what you are able, given your thinking and ability to understand and utilize the communication. That may or may not benefit you on Wall Street.

"When one hears the Voice of the Holy Spirit, they have won the lottery, and each time they choose that Voice over the voice of the world, they gain more winnings and more riches. To attempt to use that Voice to take you deeper into the illusion is something the Holy Spirit cannot do, though it will join you where you are and offer you the perception of Right-Mindedness every time you ask."

The Search for Connection

DavidPaul: Holy Spirit, what are we searching for in the world?

Holy Spirit: "God's children are seeking connection. This connection can be love and it can be experienced in other ways, including a sense of being connected to something or someone, be it a best friend, a dog, a home, a job, a cause, a partner. Everyone seeks this sense of connection, which is ultimately played out as a part of the awareness of wanting to reconnect with God or with the Oneness. There is the idea that in being connected, one will be happy, fulfilled, peaceful, and feel loved or loving.

"The striving need not be to attain more success at work or more success here and there. It is the constant striving toward that which would give them the experiences they are seeking, whether one is looking for the right job, the right relationship, and so on. There is, in the world, the ego-driven race to continue to have the next thing up, the next better this or that.

"Within a marriage, one is always seeking a better marriage within their marriage or a better marriage outside their marriage. There is always the dream of a better marriage. It is rare that the marriage is working and there is not a striving toward, or a desire for, or a disappointment because of wanting a better marriage, or wanting a better body, a better family, a better job, a better home.... There is always that striving for more. That comes from not having the peace, the love, the happiness, and the fulfillment of one's Oneness with God. They are all distractions away from the pain of not having Oneness with God."

DavidPaul: Why would we want to distract ourselves away from the pain instead of just feeling our Oneness with God?

Holy Spirit: "Why do you distract yourself away from your pain every day over a variety of issues? It is less painful, or that is what the ego would have you believe.

"The ego would have you believe that to overeat, watch TV, or drink alcohol would be less painful and easier and more rewarding somehow than to acknowledge whatever pain you are in and deal with it. For many people, it feels as if their pain is hopeless. Many people are aware that the source of their pain comes from their lack of experiencing their Oneness with God, but they have no idea how to experience their Oneness and they believe they can't fix it, so they drink. Or if one thinks that they would be happy if they just had a relationship but they cannot wave a magic wand and produce a prince in front of them, then it is easier to eat and not focus on that pain because it feels hopeless.

"There are so many dynamics that go on in this situation, such as the seeking of fleeting happiness. One experiences happiness over something such as finding the perfect dress for an important event, or finding the right man, or finding the right job and succeeding on that job, or marrying that man that they found, and so on. And when one experiences something such as finding the perfect person or marrying the perfect person, there is so much fear around losing the perfect person that they are in pain because they have determined that their happiness is based on having found this perfect person. They have made their happiness contingent upon something external, something they have no control over, something that can change and will change, something that is not of God.

"God's Love is within them and is always there unconditionally, no matter what, under any circumstances, and It is unchanging. When you put your hopes and your dreams on something external, it can only be temporary. It might be a 50-year relationship, and yet it is still temporary. And there is the fear every day that the person might die, the person might leave, the person might stop loving you, the person might start drinking, or in some way not be there. So you may have this wonderful joy and happiness while simultaneously you have all of the fear and sadness and devastation over the possibility of the relationship changing because, in fact, it can't help but change. The person can't help but change and your life can't help but change.

"One may have a child and may experience so much joy over this child in their life, but they are simultaneously constantly afraid of losing that child. What if something happens to that child? What if that child gets hurt? What if someone takes that child? This causes people to separate from that which they love, that which brings them joy and happiness, because of the fear. Anytime you believe that your happiness comes from something outside of you, it is indeed temporary. It is, in Reality, not real and it cannot be truly attained and it cannot be maintained. Ultimately, there is very little happiness upon the earth because it is brought on by external things.

"Everything that you are ultimately seeking—true happiness, peace, fulfillment, and love come from Oneness with God, come from hearing God's Voice, restoring your mind to sanity and Right-Thinking. When you live in the world in the state of mind that there are no problems, there are no victims, there is nothing wrong, there is no suffering, no blame, no attack, no injustice, no unfairness, no unkindness, and nothing unloving, when you can see it all as perfection, when you can see it all as innocence, when you can see it all as everyone in their perfect place on their path, when you can see it as God can see the world and you just have your peace and your happiness because you have chosen it, not even because you are One with God but because you just know that you can have that within you, that is when you will have true Peace, true Love, and true Happiness."

Your Expression of the Holy Spirit

DavidPaul: Holy Spirit, why do You sound different through different people?

Holy Spirit: "The Holy Spirit is the Voice for God and is a part of God's Child, so Truth and Right-Mindedness cannot be altered within God's Child. When the Holy Spirit speaks to someone within their heart and mind, the Holy Spirit communicates direct Truth to that person exactly where they are. If someone is hungry and needs food and is praying and asking about that, they will be directed on how to get food. If one is seeking spiritual fulfillment, they will be given guidance and direction on that. If one is seeking peace in a relationship, they will be given a perspective that could give them peace if they choose it. What one does with the communication, of course, is always up to them.

"When one shares the Voice of the Holy Spirit with themselves or with another or with a group, the Holy Spirit is a part of them and the sense of Truth is there. When the Holy Spirit comes through, It is coming through that person's history, experience, and mind. It becomes a more personalized expression when this happens because the Holy Spirit uses that person's personality to express Itself. The Holy Spirit will use that person's history and experiences to make examples or analogies or to tell a story. If that person, for example, is a storyteller, then the Holy Spirit would come through that person in more of a storytelling form. If the person is more left-brained and very logical and concrete, then the Holy Spirit may answer in a more specific and concrete way when communicating with someone. If one is attracted to the way someone shares the Holy Spirit, it is because that expression speaks to them. Different people will be attracted to different expressions of the Holy Spirit because of their experience, background, and belief system.

"When Candace first began sharing the Voice of the Holy Spirit, the Voice was more distinctly different than her own. As this Voice has become more integrated, or she has become more integrated into the Holy Spirit, the more the Holy Spirit sounds like her. This will be the case for everyone as they become more comfortable, familiar, and fluent in the language of the Holy Spirit. It will take on their own communication and personality traits. When one learns a new language, one brings a little of their own personality and expression to it so that when it comes out, it is more personalized than generic.

"This may cause one to be afraid that they are only listening to themselves, yet that would be the greatest revelation and the most wonderful experience one could hope for—to be so integrated with the aspect of yourself that *is* the Holy Spirit, this Voice for God, as to not be sure if it is you or the Holy Spirit speaking. If you like what you say, how you think, what you do, and how you live…and if you are able to love your neighbor, perceive the world as good and perfect, and have faith and trust that all is well—especially your union with God—you will know that you are thinking and speaking with the part of you that is the Holy Spirit. This would be a blessing indeed."

Contact Information

Thank you for joining us on this journey. We look forward to hearing how it has impacted your life, and we invite you to share your experience with us so others can be inspired by your story as well. If you would like to continue this journey with us, we post new exercises from the Holy Spirit on our website each month along with a newsletter that includes new Messages from the Holy Spirit, questions and answers regarding the book, readers' stories about hearing this Voice for themselves, and much more.

To share your story with us, hear additional communication from the Holy Spirit, or schedule a private session, speaking engagement, workshop, or retreat, please contact

Foundation for Right-Mindedness
P.O. Box 3125
Ashland, OR 97520
(541) 488-0426
www.rightmindedness.com
info@rightmindedness.com

The Foundation for Right-Mindedness, a spiritual non-profit organization, is supported by donations and gratefully accepts your tax-deductible gift.